Street Smar

(*With Proven Gam* · · *·· ··· ····g···)*

THE DEFINITIVE SUCCESS HANDBOOK FOR GENERAL MANAGERS

(…Best practices, discipline and methodology for business leaders in any field)

Authored by Paul Martino
Published by Spoke Norton Homerdome Press

Copyright ©2009 by Paul Martino
Spoke Norton Homerdome Press – Philadelphia, USA

http://**spokenorton.com**
Email: spokenorton@yahoo.com

Library of Congress Control Number: 2009901887

First Edition Printing - Philadelphia, USA
ISBN 978-0-9800917-0-0   0-9800917-0-5

PRINTED IN THE UNITED STATES OF AMERICA
Philadelphia, USA

Sincerely, Thank You!

Vic Sparaccio

Marty Donato

Doug Ramsey
Vice President and Chief Financial Officer
EXCO Resources, Inc

Ruth Anne Wood
Director of Scripting for Success^{TM} Consulting

Tom Odegaard- Senior Lecturer, Economics, Baylor University

John D. Martin- Professor of Finance and Carr P. Collins
Chair of Finance, Baylor University

Noah Hill and Jen Hill

CSC

Susan Smith
Vistage – The world's largest CEO membership organization

Dr. Lynn Lashbrook
President and Founder – Sports Management World Wide (SMWW)

Doug Miller
Owner – Dallas Stars Midget AAA Hockey Team
Partner – Texas Tornado Junior Hockey Team

Jim Bolton & Ridge Associates, Inc.

Liz Swingler and the team at Total Printing Systems

Lou Monaco

Libby Jordan

Scott Studdard

Dark Horse

Philadelphia Phillies

Foreword

Not many books are born out of passion. This book reflects Paul Martino's passion for the game of baseball. Paul has been studying the game of baseball from an early age including gathering one of the most complete New York Mets card collections ever assembled, and his USA Today recognized "Raiders of the Lost Parks" summer games tour to every MLB park. This passion ultimately led to his work with ESPN Sports Ticker as the game day statistician first for the Texas Rangers, then the New York Yankees and New York Mets. In this capacity Paul had the opportunity to interact with the players, coaches, management, media and fans providing a unique experience from which to view baseball operations and management.

Paul's educational pursuits are reflected in his book as well. The management theory and skills Paul acquired while an MBA student at Southern Methodist University's Cox School of Business, in leadership roles across the corporate enterprise at American Airlines, representing numerous vertical industries at Computer Sciences Corporation, and as a Director at a Global 500 company come together to form the basis for an effective and practical application to baseball general management.

Though it may not have direct correlation to the particulars in Paul's book, his life experiences while living, studying, working, and traveling in 45 countries undoubtedly helped shape his views on management and cross cultural issues expounded in his book.

The years of reflection and experience in baseball and management stand-out in this book written by Paul Martino. It becomes quite apparent it is a book constructed from his unabated interest and personal experiences with the subject. I would recommend this book to the sports management practitioner, student, hobbyist or fan.

J. Douglas Ramsey, Ph.D.
Vice President and Chief Financial Officer
EXCO Resources, Inc.

Dr. Ramsey is a former Adjunct Professor of Finance in the Cox School of Business at Southern Methodist University as well as a former Lecturer of Finance in the College of Business Administration at California State Polytechnic University, Pomona.

Introduction

This book is broken down into seven very different topics related to the management of Major League Baseball but founded on fundamentals, discipline, methodology, and management-view beneficial to leaders in any vertical industry.

Section 1, chapters 1-3, focuses on success criteria for baseball organizations. I provide the same methodology, discipline and philosophy for assessing the strengths, weaknesses, opportunities and threats for three MLB teams that I successfully used in my previous book, *The Official Book on the Business of Baseball General Management;* I correctly focused on the 2008 Phillies and accurately assessed specific changes the team needed to make for systemic success and to be champions. The club coincidently executed the changes, and won the World Series.

I take this same proven management discipline to provide case studies of the current Phillies, as well as the Yankees and Rangers. I selected the:

- Yankees because they are:
  - o Projected by many to be favored to win another World Series.
  - o In the public forefront, along with the Rangers, for players' banned substance use.
  - o The focus of section 2 in this book, along with the Rangers.
  - o Well, the Yankees. They have buy high – sell low and "ticker" stories to be told.

- Rangers because:
  - They have been on the opposite end of the success scale from the Yankees.
  - The long-term organization philosophy and strategy is broken. I break down the organization to uncover where they are going systemically wrong.
  - They are doing some things right. To build moment toward success I call out what they should not change.
  - To determine their current-state.
  - The team is covered in this book, along with the Yankees, due the teams being in the public spotlight for past players' use of banned substances.

- Phillies; now that they succeeded at being World Champions it is important for me to review the current-state of the organization moving forward. The team was active in the off-season building on the October momentum.

- The Phillies philosophy is very different from both the Yankees and Rangers. This book provides the reader with a solid insight of what makes the Phillies tick so differently than the others.

Section 2 is all about knocking the cover off of the ongoing saga of performance enhancement substances in Major League Baseball. This section takes on the steroid and performance enhancement meanings and issues that are being managed and covered in public under an umbrella of "illegal steroids." The real story is actually all performance enhancements under one umbrella with "illegal steroids" as only one channel of topic.

Performance enhancements, for both good and bad, are engrained in our society and daily lives of every Major League ballplayer. This book tackles all areas of legal, illegal, and MLB banned substance definitions, the management, policing, testing, and calibrating public awareness of the facts. The section first level-sets the overall issue and then looks inside the organizations seemingly most impacted, and at the stars in the spot light.

This book is not another retread of steroids, the stars who got caught and how to test players. This book provides insight in the context of a 1970s-2000s generation that has grown up with the evolution of performance improvements, both good and bad. This book also asks the questions not being asked about publicly unknown substances, masking agents, dangerous approved substances, policing and testing irregularities and then the book provides solutions for how to move forward.

At the end of the day, the purpose for this section is not for me to be right; it is for all of us, you, me, MLB management, MLBPA, media, we the Public, and the players to get it right.

This book will trigger your own memories and perceptions you had over the years and perhaps it will bring a different understanding of what you thought you understood and believed at the time. You will be sure to view the players, management, media, and performance enhancement in a clearer light. I hope this will arm you with all of the perspectives for you to develop your own questions, observations and to make your own confident judgment about MLB past, present and moving forward.

- Chapter 4:
  - Sets the ground-rules for what performance enhancements are illegal, banned and how they relate to legal and approved substances.

  - Addresses the adherence and policing conflicts and pains. MLB wants this to "just go away" but this has been building for more than 30 years and is just ramping up unless clear, manageable guidelines are set to manage the coming science and medical advancements.

  - Proposes a viable, manageable solution to defining and policing banned substances in MLB.

Chapter 5:
- Focuses on the mix of both good and bad performance enhancements through a generation, from a historical perspective. This is an American story of the times and the culture through today.

- Observes closely at the star players, and specifically at the Texas Rangers and New York Yankees. All teams are impacted. The Rangers and Yankees have been to the forefront of the publicity. You are provided with a view of what was happening to these organizations and to individual players from the 1990s through today. These two teams also competed in the playoffs three times in the 1990s with the Yankees winning all three times, and the Yankees winning the World Series each of those years. You make up your mind what you believe about who did what, when, why, for how long.

- This chapter also looks at the business and General Management pain of keeping straight what to believe, who to sign, for how long, and how much risk to take, with so many performance unknowns to base the decisions.

Section 3 is a great chapter that focuses on social styles. This chapter provides insight into all of the personality types in the clubhouse that the General Manager needs to balance. This is solid introductory insight for everyone. No matter who you are, you can gain something that hopefully excites you enough to seek out more. I highly recommend this chapter for everyone.

This section, coupled with the management chapters in the Book II section, I believe, is the building block to leadership success.

I will provide an introduction overview of Book II once you reach **Section 4**. This Book II mostly provides text book detail into:
- Sports economics
- Baseball on-field and team building strategies
- Management building blocks of ethics, communication, expectation setting, and living with a strong "ticker."

In summary, this book, *Street Smart Sports Management*, will provide you with:

- Street smart, real-world management methodology, discipline, philosophy and techniques:
  - For anyone in any business
  - Directly pertaining to Major League Baseball

- Baseball specific insight into:
  - Performance enhancements
  - Team organizations
  - On-field and off strategies for success
  - Labor economics

Sidebar: With each of my publications I share reading recommendations with you from my library. In addition to the sports books and links in Appendix A, I recommend these also in my library:

- *People Styles at Work*, Robert Bolton and Dorothy Grover Bolton
- *Super Crunchers*, Ian Ayres
- *Ice to the Eskimos*, Jon Spoelstra
- *Break Into Sports Through Ticket Sales*, Mark Washo
- *Marketing Outrageously*, Jon Spoelstra
- *Outliers*, Malcolm Gladwell
- *Sway*, Ori Brafman and Rom Brafman

BOOK I

Section 1

Rangers, Yankees, Phillies Case Studies

Chapter 1:

Texas Rangers– It's Not Payroll, It's Pitching

The baseball experts favorite "whisper" team in 2009 has been the Rangers of the weak AL West. Just as likely to finish near the bottom of the American League power rankings, the team is getting attention for their signing of young position players, balanced with promising pitchers in their minor league system.

I have a tremendous respect for the Texas Rangers organization. The employees throughout the organization from Tom Hicks down throughout the entire organization represent the highest class, respect, friendliness and "southern hospitality." They have created a tremendous atmosphere to watch a baseball game. The Ballpark in Arlington provides a relaxing, pleasant, fun, almost…well, picnic-like environment. The team represents the great down to earth, quality of life that the DFW area represents.

The restaurants, food stands, and suites are great, it's clean and has a unique field that makes it a neat trip for fans across the country to come and visit. Kids can run onto the post centerfield grass to chase down homeruns, there is a waffle ball field, and it has a great baseball museum. It is safe. I recommend baseball fans and their families everywhere to plan a trip to the Ballpark in Arlington. Red Sox, Yankees, Phillies, Cubs and other fans can come on down and wear their hometown t-shirts and caps without fear of being pelted and harassed. The games are also exciting. The Rangers have offensive teams and they sure do give up a lot of runs.

Travel outside of Texas-Oklahoma and this bright organization is a well kept secret. Until recently, when I raise the topic of the Rangers, when I am outside of the South-Southwest, people usually begin to talk hockey and I need to tell them, not the New York Rangers, I'm talking about the Texas Rangers.

I am not trying to slip in a joke here, I'm serious. Even in the California bay area-San Jose and San Diego-LA-Anaheim areas where great hockey strides were made, people reply in terms of the New York Rangers. Even in Florida where Tampa Bay has made hockey inroads. I find this especially peculiar because hockey is not exactly lighting up Sports Center and the magazine stands with a wealth of publicity.

Recently, however, I have noticed two more frequent, troubling responses; either about steroids, Canseco, A-Rod, Palmeiro, and others, or "that losing team in Texas."

The [Texas] Rangers want to win. The team has a scouting department that perpetually finds players who can flat-out hit. The Rangers always seem to have offensive stars rising from the minor leagues. The Rangers will also spend the money if that would bring a winning team. The team has tried to win, spent the money, and been somewhat burned first by the steroid era and second by an organizational philosophy that dates back to the 1970s of offense over pitching and defense.

In my previous book I mentioned that in the mid-1980s I sat in the bleachers at Arlington Stadium and fans were discussing how the Rangers would never be World Champions because they did not believe in pitching. I wondered why the casual fans had figured this out but the Rangers couldn't or wouldn't.

Now it is 2009 and the topic is still the same; Rangers don't have pitching. The Texas Rangers will never win the World Series until they embrace pitching as the leading success factor.

The team recently made a significant stride in changing this philosophy by bringing on local hero Nolan Ryan to bring pitching knowledge and hopefully discipline to the organization. The Rangers are supposed to have a solid crop of solid pitchers in their farm system that will bring the major league team to credibility and championship caliber competitiveness but newspaper archives are a library full of hearing this from the Rangers over the past thirty years. It is time for the team to prove it. This is also quite a load to place on these minor league pitchers.

Ironically, this talk of Nolan Ryan's Rangers minor league pitching wealth reminds me of the last truly Hall-of-Fame minor league greatness of Nolan Ryan, Tom Seaver, Jon Matlack, Jerry Koosman, and Tug McGraw team built by the New York Mets. Anything less on scale and I believe the Rangers need to figure out how to sign some quality free agents and how to make better quality trades.

What really troubles me though is how the topic has moved to, "the Rangers can't get or keep good pitching because it is too hot in Arlington. It is just too hot down there in the Texas sun."

Respectfully, I need to shoot holes into this argument like I am in a shootout at the Tombstone OK Corral, for the tough love sake of the Rangers baseball fans and to put a tombstone on this argument. Hopefully this will get the fans some PITCHING.

Yes Texas Rangers, I am calling you out for a good 'ole fashioned draw. I'm ready, guns a blazing, because I want to see you win. Get your best excuses and bring them out to home plate. I'll bring mine out to the pitching mound. At high noon, when it's good and hot, let's cover this temperature argument. The fans are getting burned but it is not by the Texas sun. Ready…draw!

- The Rangers play 162 games;
  - 81 games are at home.

- Only roughly 40 games are at home in the summer (June, July, and August).

- Of those 40 games, which the opposition needs to provide a pitcher too, only TWO games will be played during the day in June, July and August COMBINED. Two games.

- Now, let's say each day game is a treacherous four hours (longer than average). Each team has to take the field for two hours. The starting pitcher is out of the game in the 6th inning or roughly 1hr and 15 minutes of work.

- Each relief pitcher goes out there for roughly 20 minutes.

- The same starting pitcher does not pitch both day games in Arlington. Essentially 50% of the Rangers pitching staff are tasked with pitching 1hr and 15 minutes in the Texas daytime sun per year.

- Yes, it is admittedly hot during these 38 night games in Arlington. While the average high during the day is in the mid 90s, it is still a hot 80s many nights.

However, the Cubs, Yankees, and Phillies play most of their home games during the midday summer sun. Try pitching under the Wrigley Field, Yankee Stadium or Citizens Bank Park summer sun; when the temperature is also in the 80s and 90s. You know where the Phillies fans are during the day if they are not at the Phillies game? They are at the Jersey shore beach, because it is so darned hot! The reason why the girls are walking around in bikinis and millions are at the beach in the northeast is because it is summer hot there too.

- It is hot everywhere. The tough teams win because they win during the "dog days of summer." This term was created long before the Rangers became a franchise, before air conditioning, and before plane travel became normal. This term was created when a pitcher usually pitched complete games more times than not, in thick, heavy uniforms, without Gatorade.

- The Dallas Cowboys, high school and college football players throughout Texas and the throughout the country are playing football in heavy pads and uniforms, beating each others' brains out in the same August heat, for hours without a dugout to hang out in for half the game or after maybe an hour or so of total work in the sun, during 2-a-days, running sprints.

- Nolan Ryan came to the Rangers in 1989 at the age of 42 and pitched there for 5 more years. In that time Nolan Ryan managed to pitch over 150 innings 4 times, over 200 innings twice, strike out over 10 batters per game 3 years straight including over 300 batters year, pitch 2 no-hitters. At age 46, on the hot summer August 4, game in Arlington, Nolan Ryan had enough energy to punch out Robin Ventura. I'm sure if Nolan Ryan can pitch throughout his 40s in Arlington back in 1989-93 then pitchers in their 20s can pitch there today.

- One more player example of many more, with the point made; Charlie Hough arrived at 32 and pitched successfully, winning 139 games over 10 years with the Rangers.

- There is a reason why they call Atlanta, "Hotlanta." As the world found out during the Olympics, it is hot in Atlanta in the summer. The Braves managed to support the MLB best pitching staff for nearly 20 years.

The second excuse given annually for the Rangers shortfalls is that the team is in a small market, unable to compete with large market franchises. The evidence does not support this argument. Without getting too granular, from a 30k foot view:

- Dallas is the 9th largest city in the country.
- Fort Worth is the 17th largest city in the country.
- Arlington is the 50th largest city in the country.
- The 6.1 million people in the Dallas-Arlington-Fort Worth metropolitan area is the 4th largest metropolitan area in the country and first in Texas (over Houston).

Compare this to, say, the Atlanta metropolitan area is ranked 33rd in the country and the city itself is ranked roughly 33rd in the country.

Meanwhile, the Texas Rangers 2008 payroll was 21st (circa $67million) among MLB teams, roughly a full $20million behind the Milwaukee Brewers, Houston Astros, nearly $40million behind the Atlanta Braves. The Rangers spent a full $30million less than the World Champion Philadelphia Phillies.

If DFW is a metropolitan area that does not support its sports teams then the Rangers might have some intangible argument. The Rangers attendance was 1,946,000; roughly 2million fans, ranking 25th at 24,000plus per game. However, the Rangers finished 21 games out of 1st place after finishing 19 games out the year before. This caused the Rangers attendance to drop to a 20 year low. Don't blame the fans for lack of support.

The Rangers had an unsuccessful product in 2008. The team spent that way. $68million is fine if you have Tampa Bay talent. If not, then spend the market bearing $98million if you want fans to show up. You can get a whole lot of pitching for $30million. You can get a whole lot for just $20million. The Rangers had a 5+ERA all 2008, a full run over the rest of the league. It was worse than that; the team was a leader in errors, meaning they gave up a whole to of runs that didn't even hit the team ERA. Here is a history of how solid the Rangers fan base has been. Take a close look from the mid-90s through 2008 and see how long a fan-base kept the faith until the 4th lousy year in a row:

YR	W	L	GB	Att (rounded)	avg att (rnd)	rank of 14
1996	90	72	-	2,900,000	36k	3rd
1997	77	85	13	2,950,000	36k	4th
1998	88	74	-	2,950,000	36k	4th
1999	95	67	-	2,775,000	34k	5th
2000	71	91	20.5	2,800,000	32k	5th
2001	73	89	43	2,850,000	35k	5th
2002	72	90	31	2,350,000	29k	6th
2003	71	91	25	2,000,000	26k	7th
2004	89	73	3	2,500,000	31k	6th
2005	79	83	16	2,500,000	31k	6th
2006	80	82	13	2,400,000	29k	7th
2007	75	87	19	2,350,000	29k	8th
2008	79	83	21	1,950,000	24k	11th

I can tell you from talking to many fans that they probably would have gone to games in 2008 had they seen the team spend some money on some players but that they figured why should they show up to see a bad team that the ownership didn't even invest in. Let's look at the team salary over the years to see if this fan perception or valid or if there is a bigger story:

YR	W	L	GB	Att (rounded)	avg att (rounded)	Att rank out of 14	Payroll (rounded)
1996	90	72	-	2,900,000	36k	3rd	$36million
1997	77	85	13	2,950,000	36k	4th	$50million
1998	88	74	-	2,950,000	36k	4th	$55million
1999	95	67	-	2,775,000	34k	5th	$81million
2000	71	91	20.5	2,800,000	32k	5th	$70million
2001	73	89	43	2,850,000	35k	5th	$88million
2002	72	90	31	2,350,000	29k	6th	$106million
2003	71	91	25	2,000,000	26k	7th	$103million
2004	89	73	3	2,500,000	31k	6th	$55million
2005	79	83	16	2,500,000	31k	6th	$55million
2006	80	82	13	2,400,000	29k	7th	$68million
2007	75	87	19	2,350,000	29k	8th	$68million
2008	79	83	21	1,950,000	24k	11th	$68million

Whether the Rangers spent $36million or $81million they were able to take first place and the fan base remained relatively static at circa 35,000.

Then whether the team spent $55million or $106million they usually landed double digits out of first place, and the fans showed up at roughly 30,000. The combined increase in attendance and poor results in 2001, along with the gradual decline in attendance is assumed to be the fan support for signing A-Rod and then Juan Gonzalez, coupled with the realization that the team was a big loser.

The fans continued to show up in 2004 when they nearly won the division until 2008 after 4 years of losing and 5th year of ownership conservative player acquisitions finally turned the fans away. There are two sides to this story; the fans became jaded but the ownership appears, through these facts, that they got jaded by their doubling of the payroll only to see a first place team fall a devastating 43 and 31 games out of first place.

The real story within these numbers is a bigger picture than one of a supposedly small market with dwindling fan base coupled with a poor geographic location. The real story is in profit maximization coupled with an offensive philosophy:

1. Profit Maximization
   The team leans toward profit maximizing but spends when the team is positioned to win or begins to slide. The team tried to take a first place team to the Championship level by spending more money and got badly burned so the ownership pulled back. Attendance stayed high during the losing years, and even almost came in first in MLB's weakest division so it continued to minimize payroll. The team became complacent because it was able to profit maximize without any direct relation between success and spending over 12 year time frame.

2. Offensive philosophy
   The Rangers misinterpreted as disconnect the success link to investment results when they won with a $55million payroll and lost with a $103million payroll. The reason why the Rangers did not win in the 2000s was because it returned to the long term team philosophy of spending the payroll on offense and neglecting the pitching. The team in the 1990s had strong offense and pitching.

The Rangers lost to the eventual World Champion Yankees in 1996, 98, and 99. Instead of building on the team bottom roster 10% it began to dismantle the team. Instead of building on the fundamentals that got them there, the team began to self destruct under its offensive philosophy.

Now, Tom Hicks has been vocal about the money he lost on Juan Gonzalez and the losses incurred with A-Rod. That said, he purchased the team in 1998 for $250million and the team last in 2008, depending on the estimate, to be at circa $320million (actually dropping $15-$50million over the past 4 years as they held back payroll and the team continued double digit positions behind first place.

In order to succeed, and make folks believe, the team needs to reverse both the recent pitching failures and a long-standing organizational philosophical history. Baseball is a game of statistics and legacy. The current Rangers must live with the pitching legacy of its own creation:

- 1982 - Ron Darling (pitching) and Walt Terrell (pitching) to the Mets for Lee Mazzilli (I'd say for hitting but he hit .228 in 1981).

- 1983 – Rick Honeycutt for Dave Stewart (the Dodgers also consider this one of their worst trades). What made this trade so bad for the Rangers is that he wound up still winning the AL ERA title that year, and because this All-Star on pace for 20 wins was traded right before the mid-August showdown between the second place Rangers and the first place White Sox. The team threw in the towel for the future right before the series that could propel them to first place.

- 1978 - Dave Righetti for Sparky Lyle (and other players in the trade). The team can be defended for what looked like a good deal at the time but we are looking at over 30 years of pitching legacy here and this turned out to be a disaster of a trade (and I had this extra bullet to shoot, to convince this Rangers team to give Nolan Ryan everything he asks for).

The team, I believe, is caught up in a payroll vs. wins to losses profit maximization, instead of payroll offense to pitching philosophy. If the team invests in pitching, the consistent wins will come, and the revenue will rise. I believe that if given the chance, with adequate investment, Nolan Ryan will build this pitching staff and then the team will win and the fans will come and the team value will shoot upward too.

For the 2009 Texas Rangers, once again, it's not about the payroll they'll need to live with; it's about the pitching situation they created. It's not about the weather; it's about the pitching.

RANGERS SCORESHEET

Criteria	RYG	Success 1L-20H	elevator speech
Owner Maximizers	Yellow	14	I am convinced the team will make needed moves and increase payroll if positioned to win. Recent lack of success negatively reflects on team. Have building blocks to surprise West. Need to make happen.
Owner Contract risk	Yellow	14	Mr. Hicks wants to win. Team direction, not risk is the issue. However, recent signing could be sign headed for green.
Transaction Philosophy:			
Buy low, sell high	Red	8	A-Rod represents team lack of confidence in and big picture moves. 1^{St} bad signing, 2nd painful trade. No sustained direction yet.
Value draft picks vs. free agents	Red	8	All over the map. Free agents one year, trades the next, farm for future the next. No direction. Supposed to have strong pitchers in farm system but been there too many times before. Need MLB proof now.
Improve through player changes	Red	10	I would say no direction but each move seems to sink them lower in the standings; direction downward. However, Rangers could surprise people with recent signings.
Stock of rare skilled players	Yellow	12	Recent signings in effort to keep young stars for long future, rumor of strong pitchers in minors but limited credibility. Always find the stud young offensive players. Counting on Nolan Ryan.
Forget pocket cost	Red	10	Schizophrenic. Blaming failures on being a small market team is not backed by fact.
Adjust to division and league	Red	8	Last place in the weakest division in baseball. August becomes Cowboys season.
Don't be Yankees farm system	Yellow	12	Player changes make The Ballpark in Arlington like Grand Central Station
Trade through strength	Red	10	Blame lack of pitching improvement on the Texas heat is weak. Small market mentality puts team at trading disadvantage.
Balance of needs with budget	Red	10	Pitching and defense wins championships. Known for offense.
General Management	Red	6	Daniels has not been successful. This is put up or step aside time.
Scouting	Green	17	Strong offensive tendency supposed to have found pitching- need proof because team can't sign proven pitchers.
Field Management	Yellow	13	Tough to beat up on managers who recently were set up to fail. Need to see results now.

Chapter 2:

Yankees – Crossroads in a Changing Game

Unfortunately, the driving factors for the Yankees success on the field in 2009 is founded less on actual players than on three core economic factors and three supporting variables:
1. The unpredictable driven by the historic USA bear market.
2. Profit Maximization vs. Victory Maximization.
3. Red Sox Buy Low-Sell High vs. Yankees Buy High-Sell Low.
4th, 5th and 6th driving the Yankees success are the new stadium, player ticker, and talent.

In order to address how the Yankees will fair over the next couple of years, you the reader and I need to be on the same baseline backstop. We can agree to disagree on my interpretation of the facts but we at least need to use the same facts as reference points.

MLB Economic Backstop

A lot has been made about the Yankees payroll. Briefly, the public perception is about as off from realities as the view on performance enhancements. Yes, the Yankees payroll is the highest in MLB. However, cost of living based on taxes, housing and other factors, is quite different between New York City and Dallas; New York to the casual US citizen is 80% higher than Dallas, Texas.

Folks living in Dallas may take issue with my cost of living comparison but trust me, I base my value on cost of living from first hand experience. I moved from Dallas to New York with an ex-employer. When the cost of living adjustment promised to me was not kept, my stay in New York became a brief one. I completely understand why the Yankees payroll is higher than the rest of the league in hard numbers but relatively close to the middle of the pack in relative terms:

- A person who makes $29,000 in Dallas needs $50,000 to live equally in New York City. The New York City middle class is actually nearing the $175,000 line.
- A Yankees player who makes $10,000,000 is making the same salary value as the Rangers player who makes $5,600,000.
- This means that the Yankees $200,000,000 team salary base is equal to $113,000,000 to the Texas Rangers.
- The New York Yankees also paid $27million in luxury tax to teams like the Texas Rangers in 2008.
- In hard numbers 13 MLB teams are projected to spend over $100million in 2009. Most of the uproar over the Yankees is from teams that spent circa $50million in 2008, roughly half or less spending than even the average MLB team. Plus, the bottom teams made profits from the Yankees salary tax.

For another book, my argument is that Wilmington, Delaware, Trenton, New Jersey, and Austin, Texas cities all have minor league ball clubs. If teams at the bottom of the Major Leagues have such a small market that they cannot compete with modern society then they should compete with the other successful cities that have minor league teams.

If you can't run with the dogs then stay on the porch.

Yes, the Yankees payroll is higher even on cost of living balance with other teams but:

- The difference is much closer than when comparing in real terms.
- Yankees attendance is through the roof, cable ratings high, and they are profitable.
- Merchandise alone pays for individual star player salaries. A-Rod was relatively paid for in merchandise alone after only 1 month of the trade.
- The $10million team George Steinbrenner bought is now worth over $1billion.
- The Yankees essentially accomplished the baseball version of what the Dallas Cowboys accomplished in merchandise value.
- The Yankees success factor is the World Series victory while teams on the other extreme determine success by net profit. Other teams balance net profit with winning record.

The Rangers spent circa $68million (22nd in spending, significantly behind the likes of Milwaukee, Cincinnati and Detroit). This is more of an indictment against the Rangers (profit maximizers) than anything the Yankees (victory maximizers) are doing that overloads the balance of competition. The Rangers actually took a greater advantage of the market conditions than the Yankees.

I would indicate to the outraged observers that the Yankees spending in 2009 actually decreased from 2005 and 2008 but this could change on any given day so I'll just make reference that this was the case in February.

The USA Economic Impact on Major League Baseball Pennants & Victory Maximizers Historic Opportunity

Throughout my publications and later in this book, I detail how the victory maximizers have a competitive advantage over profit maximizing teams in terms of World Series Championships, while profit maximizing teams generate greater single season profits in general, but ultimately the victory maximizing teams overall value is much greater than the profit maximizers.

Other factors such as ultimate success at player valuation play a great role in single season successes but revenue is the dominant mechanism in gaining players who do not rise from within the organization. The New York Yankees organization is the poster child for victory maximization. The Boston Red Sox currently run second.

This coming couple of years is clearly in favor of any team that dedicates itself to win the World Series. The reason is that MLB revenue is expected to be down due to the significant loss of corporate related revenues, the spike in layoffs, lack of consumer confidence, and the historic level of global decline.

In real terms individual teams are reluctant to sign high priced players, they want fewer years contract risk, are conservative in signing any player with any mental, physical, personal, family, marriage or age related issues of any kind. Any rumor of a player taking illegal or banned performance enhancement drugs have left players on the sideline.

Importantly, once the season begins, don't get too attached to any player in any town USA because there will be little tolerance for any player not performing in any respect as expected when signed. Additionally, any team that starts low and drops out of the race is going to be more inclined to dump payroll as standings and attendance drops. Teams will be very reluctant to hold onto lowering asset values, players included, due to concerns about organization stability and profitability.

The victory maximizing teams throughout the year, mid-season, at the trading deadline, and even up to September 1 are likely to find many bargains never seen before in baseball. Even after September 1, teams can attain great trade bargains to position the team for success the following season.

No industry is safe during the greatest financial crisis since the Great Depression and individual MLB teams who do not see a chance to win over the next few years, or who find themselves unexpectedly uncompetitive will choose to ride out the downturn by dumping greater revenue players.

At the top of the list will be the Yankees, possibly the Mets who are desperate to get the "roadrunner" monkey off their back of historic collapses to the Phillies, perhaps the Phillies who may add a needed pitcher, and other teams who may find success, higher revenues and see an opportunity to add that one missing link.

Every team with any kind of speed, hitting, power, pitching, defense, bench, relief, or specific utilization role player shortfall will be able to fill their need at any point throughout the next couple of seasons unprecedented in modern times due to the impact of the USA economy on individual franchises and their immediate level of success, coupled with fan and corporate support limitations.

At the end of the day the Yankees and Red Sox are positioned to be the greatest winners over the next two years in the American League, and the Phillies, Mets, perhaps the Cubs are the favorites in the National League.

This does not mean that these teams have everything wrapped up. The Rays, Angels, White Sox, Indians, Cardinals could surprise. Even the Giants could make a string of surprise moves over the year that gets them to the playoffs. As Earl Weaver once said, he could get his team to the playoffs but it is all luck after that.

Notice the low payroll Rays are included. This team committed itself to internal player development to compete and have a solid returning team. Victory maximizing can be short term as well as long term. In addition, victory maximization is not always determined by payroll. Victory maximization also has degrees of value. The Yankees and Red Sox are the extremes.

Any team that wants to emphasize victory maximization is positioned now better than any time since the 1970s. This unique opportunity comes once in a generation. Any team can compete if they are risk averse enough to make a run for the pennant.

This is the "Day of the Victory Maximizers." Any team that cannot run in this volatile climate needs to stay on the porch.

From a revenue perspective, the Yankees are the favorites. From a fiscal and business smart perspective, the Red Sox are the favorites. Let's discuss this buy high-sell low vs. buy low-sell high situation between the Yankees and Red Sox next.

Buy High, Sell Low vs. Buy Low, Sell High

Overall the Yankees:
1. Yes, spend more than other teams but by a closer real cost margin than it seems.
2. The Yankees need to spend more because they make so many high dollar signing mistakes. If they made a higher percentage of quality signings the team payroll would be much lower.
3. While the team has strong potential with the pitching, it should be in better position to win based upon the salary structure.

The New York Yankees were anointed the World Series by many fans and some experts due to all of their off-season signings. I believe the signings got the Yankees to compete with Red Sox and Rays (teams with equal pitching to the Yankees; the three favorites in the AL have the three best pitching staffs).

The Yankees by no stretch of imagine, short of all of the moves they'll ultimately make during the course of the next couple of seasons, have anything locked up. The team can win the World Series but, at the same time) may not win a Wild Card, b) have enough holes that it looks like they got shot by a lot of the bullets fired in the previous chapter on the Texas Rangers.

Before we discuss some specifics, I point out that the Red Sox spend less than the Yankees but still are in the top MLB percentile. The Red Sox also know the value of buy low-sell high. The team is committed to its players and willing to sign aging players, at the right price.

Red Sox greats, Pedro Martinez, Johnny Damon and Omar Garciaparra are examples of the team accurate valuations of older players. Wise trades that brought them the likes of Jason Bay, Beckett and others, as well as a strong minor league system allows the team to spend less than the Yankees and produce equal or recently better results than the Yankees.

In contrast, the Yankees signing shortfalls are legendary and well documented. The recent Jason Giambi, Johnny Damon, and many other signings are example of how the team signs players at their peak, lose draft picks in many cases, and get little, disappointing, or no value for their signings.

The team often makes trades for players because they are at their peak but many turn out to be disappointing. I would argue that Ted Lilly and Mariano Soriano would have brought greater results at far less price than Weaver and A-Rod. The team just has a knack of buying high and selling low, at the cost of their minor league system.

One reason for the Red Sox success has been their ability to judge a player beyond the Bill James sabermetrics to come up with the players with a ticker. For example, Jason Varitek, made it clear to A-Rod who was boss, Curt Schilling welcomed going to the Red Sox to take the Yankees down.

A-Rod has fizzled under pressure, Giambi had his issues, Abreu, like Giambi and A-Rod, had great stats but no real "Paul O'Neill" sign of competitive anger. These guys just haven't had that "Ticker."

The recent Yankees have been too "nice." Even Andy Pettitte is missing that air of dominance.

I would not have placed Mike Mussina in the category of Yankees "larvadness" (not in dictionary, it means how it sounds). However, who retires 30 games, 2 seasons shy of 300 wins? Mussina won 20 games. The Yankees are free wheelin' spending, added gold-glover, offensive star in Mark Teixeira, added relief pitching; all that essentially guarantee you 300 immortal level career 300 wins and…you RETIRE? What is behind this story we don't know about?

This team, from a ticker perspective is no match for Red Sox or Yankees of the 1990s. This team flat out looks slow, lethargic, and average when going up against the Rays. Where is the speed, the hustle, the competitive anger? Where is the ticker?

The hallway between the Yankees clubhouse to the dugout used to say, "There is no substitute for Victory – Douglas MacArthur." I suspect the Yankees took it down because they saw they had a team of underachieving players who did not live by that Goose Gossage, Thurman Munson, Sparky Lyle, Lou Piniella, Paul O'Neill, Reggie Jackson competitiveness.

Throughout my books I emphasize the importance of the "ticker" that doesn't show up in the statistics. Joe Torre was recently on the MLB Channel. He used the term "ticker" when discussing his disagreements with some Yankees signings. This is leadership-speak of saying the Yankees recently were less than successful in separating pure statistics with the winning competitive anger intangible.

Whether or not the Yankees win the World Series that they are favored to win will change from day to day with their next signings but the team over recent years has lacked the competitive anger to seal the deal. They have been talented enough but just lacked that intangible that has led the Red Sox to victory.

At the end of the day, the laundry list of players the Yankees bought high and sold low has been equal to the list that the Red Sox bought low and sold high. This is the neutralizer to overcome the top spending team in MLB.

Buying high, selling low is how a Victory Maximizing team can spend $200million a year and have no World Series to show for it, and not even a playoff berth.

Let's look at the Yankees – current state. Why are experts guaranteeing World Series success while I have my doubts, beyond this "lacking a ticker" thing? Here is a high level view to through caution to the wins.

What my observations call out in one elevator pitch is, it remains to be seen that this team can run with the dogs. This team has as much risk of sitting in the bleachers in the off-season as winning it with a homerun into the new stadium porch. The team got it right in going after pitching. It's about pitching and defense. Along with the pitching they got a solid first baseman. This puts the Yankees in the championship competition level. Any injuries or lackluster performance will be addressed by additional moves.

That said this team should not have as many weaknesses as it does:

- The Yankees outfield – 3 full positions in the field and in the lineup (a full 33% of the lineup) - has been for years, comparably, extremely weak. They are positioned to struggle.

  The lack of power and poor defensive performance is alarming for any team let alone a team positioning $200million to win the World Series. This has been an ongoing mess that the team previously tried to correct with buy high guys like Abreu, Damon and others. Too much expectation put on Cabrera.

- The team looks slow. There are no situational Mickey Rivers, Willie Randolph spark plug combinations.

- Mark Teixeira will be a solid clutch hitting plus to go with Derek Jeter but A-Rod is a statistical juggernaut while not Reggie Jackson or Thurman Munson or even Craig Nettles.

- Second base and overall bench are weak. I like Cano but this team should have a lot more to show for its money that isn't happening. An injury to Jeter, A-Rod, Posada, or Teixeira, and it has serious problems. The overall offensive roster is scary weak.

- Posada is a great player but injuries are setting in at the toughest position in baseball.

- The Yankees definitely bought high in pitching. The team can win the World Series with this pitching staff. However, there is a significant amount of risk. They need to hope that Burnett does not return to injuries and Sabathia can stay healthy under that physical and New York pressure weight.

If the Baseball Gods empowered me with the powers, I would trade this outfield with the 1971, 82-80 Yankees in a heartbeat. I would take Bobby Murcer, Felipe Alou, Roy White, and Ron Swoboda in the outfield to join the current Yankees team, and I'd being saving up my money for the next Yankees WS showing. This current Yankees outfield, with this bench; I'm not sure the Yankees don't need to make continued improvements throughout the year.

The Yankees now have the aura and excitement advantage of the gorgeous new Yankee Stadium. I was in awe at the presence this stadium has on its own. I felt the presence of Babe Ruth, Lou Gehrig, Joe DiMaggio, Phil Rizzuto, and Yogi Berra of Yankees yore. I've sat in the Yankee stadium of the '60s, the renovated Yankee stadium, and this new stadium is blood rushing exciting.

However, historically, teams often have an adjustment period of up to one year when moving to a new stadium. The Yankees may be different because they have so many player changes and because you can't add much to the New York pressure cooker that isn't already there. The stadium is one of those intangibles that will have to play out as another Yankees advantage or adjustment.

At the end of the day, post George Steinbrenner, the Yankees legacy, reputation, and career of their GM is on the line. The team can win. In the historically best day for the Victory Maximizers, the Yankees will need a leadership overhaul if they cannot win over the next few years.

YANKEES SCORE SHEET

Criteria	RYG	success 1L-20 H	elevator speech
Owner Maximizers	Green	18	Only success is winning the World Series. Doesn't always spend wisely.
Owner Contract risk	Green	18	Takes significant derivative risk Recommend signing strong outfielder Very weak outfield for way too much $$
Transaction Philosophy:			
Buy low, sell high	Red	8	Tendency to sign last year's star for top $, mixed results. At times cannot unload the bad signings. Examples: should have kept Lilly, Soriano, not signed Damon, Giambi
Value draft picks vs. free agents	Yellow	12	Recently improved but red previously. That could change any day to day. Wise longer term signings for younger free agents recently to limit draft pick losses.
Improve through player changes	Yellow	14	The upside is they do change when needed but OF is too weak and sometimes make rotisserie changes that back fire.
Stock of rare skilled players	Yellow	12	Teams like the Rays made the Yankees look sluggish. No Mickey Rivers type sparkplugs. No Paul O'Neill type anger.
Forget pocket cost	Green	20	Bottomless money pit. The poster child for forgetting pocket cost.
Adjust to division and league	Green	16	Have frustrated the Red Sox for years and divisional winning streak snapped in 2008. Risk of yellow. Epstein-James Sox era major inroads to reverse generations' trend.
Don't be Yankees farm system	Yellow	15	That's good and bad. Recently they've held on to their young stars. Limited patience on young players. They remove failed players. Bad free agent signings lose draft picks.
Trade through strength	Green	16	When you have $$, risk averse, young players, stars, ready to eat contracts you are flexible to drive many deals. Opposition players approve trades to come to winner.
Balance of needs with budget	Yellow	13	When you have a $200million budget… Outfield doesn't reflect budget
General Management	Yellow	15	Toughest job in some ways, luckiest in others. Has to deal with advisors. At end of the day not enough to show for $200million
Scouting	Green	17	Consistent strategy and discipline.
Field Management	Green	17	Knows the game. Strong character. Catcher attitude and view of the game.

Chapter 3:

Phillies – Vision, Discipline, Commitment

While the Yankees have been pitching smart but buy high-sell low for less than team sparkplugs over recent years, and the Rangers have been misers with solid offense and legendary "buy no pitching" philosophy, the Phillies have maintained a buy-low, limit risk, balance of pitching, offense, defense, and speed approach. The team has been successful through investment in their minor league system, strong coaching, and scouting. The payoff for the Phillies was the World Championship while the Yankees and Rangers stayed home.

The Phillies holdback before 2008 was the ownership risk adverse tendency to hold salary that landed the team one or two players shy of first place. The ownership did its job in 2008, opened the wallet fiscally responsible enough to get the club over the hump. The management and players did not disappoint. Brad Lidge was near perfect with 41 of 41 save opportunities and 92ks in 69 innings. Quietly, even the Matt Stairs pick up turned to gold.

The Philadelphia Phillies are in a historic position to turn the National League East into the modern remake of the "Roadrunner."

Two years in a row the Mets improved its team, positioned to win the division right up to September, but the team turned into a Wile E Coyote leadership bought ACME product.

This third off-season the Phillies did a solid job by adding Raul Ibanez and little else. Ownership increased budget again in 2009 to keep current key players and improve the team to a point that they can be in the lead going into September instead of blasting the guns to the finish line.

The team won last year with a .255 so they really are positioned to perform much better than last year. Ibanez is a consistent .290 hitter, he is from New York so the bet is he can step right into the Phillies-Mets pressure cooker, and he is tailor made to fit into the workman-like Phillies team atmosphere. The only downside is that one Phillies weak area is with offensive strikeouts and Raul strikes out circa 100 times yearly. His 20-30 homers and consistency, driving in 100 runs yearly could soften that aspect.

My one concern is not about talent; it is with the increased natural risk of injury to Jamie "Father Time" Moyer. He counts on pitching vs. power so he can do it. It's just that darned reality that nature hits us over the head with when we approach 50. The back end is a staff of committee led by Blanton, Happ, Kendrick, Park, and others could be enough. If by July it turns out not to be quite enough, the Phillies management will need to present a strong, wise business case for a sure-to-be available pitcher from another team in this economic downturn that the ownership can have confidence enough to pull the trigger. The Phillies did what they needed to move beyond 1-2 players short and are sure to be concerned about not steering too high in payroll now. This may be a mute point if the 4-5 slots, mid relief staff-by-committee and Moyer hold up.

The Phillies young arms could counter the depth risk, and now that the Phillies have won the World Series you have to put total trust and faith that the organization has great confidence in the farm system that has earned trust over recent very prosperous years.

Meanwhile the Mets did an A+ off-season job filling the relief staff holes so this season points to a very exciting season. The Mets also know they were able to win the head-to-head series last year. With the impressively overhauled relief staff and returning Wagner, this should be an exciting summer.

That said, improved staff and their head-to-head improvements aside, it's the Phillies who won the East again, and then won under the pressure of NL titles and World Series. For this reason, it's the Mets who have the 100% load of the pressure this season. The Phillies have to prove they can do it again and preferably easier but it's the Mets who need to prove they won't cave in historical fashion. If they run into injuries, Wagner doesn't come back, the outfield doesn't produce or a host of other risks, then the improved Phillies may have a new cartoon made after them. Beep! Beep!

Overall, from an organizational perspective the Phillies seem to be in the driver seat in this economy. Before last season fans, Wall Street, main stream media, and I were critical of the team maintaining a long-standing, heart-breaking one or two player short of a World Series budget. The team was so close.

Ownership followed up the World Series season with an extremely busy and committed off-season by sealing the deal with the key players on the team:

- Hamels - 3 years, circa $20million
- Howard - 3 years, circa $55million
- Moyer – 2 years, circa $13million
- Plus a half dozen other players locked up

I do not profess in any way shape or form that my detailed analysis of one team in my book – the Phillies – had anything to do with the Phillies success last year. That said the ownership and management needs to be commended for hearing the public outcry and making the very changes that I detailed (and it did read my book):

1. The team increased the payroll by circa $10million.
2. The team solidified the relief staff with some of the extra $10million.
3. The team made strategic moves at midseason and pre-September 1 for specialized role players.

Even more promising is that the team payroll increased again this year. The team recognized its opportunity to be World Champions, they increased the budget, and they made the right player decisions with that added budget. The entire organization chemistry, vision, disciplines and philosophy is now a model for other MLB teams.

The Phillies built an extended success structure of strong scouting, drafting, and player development. They had one missing link and that was some more ownership assistance. The ownership erased this weakness last season and to start off 2009. The management and players proved the trust was worth it. Post steroid era, the Phillies are in position to succeed in this new on-field game. They need to stay the buy low-sell high but continue to improve course to hold onto this success. Alternative "Art of the Long View" pitching options need to be proactively developed in case of any sign of cracks.

Regarding Phillies success the special contagious fan energetic support needs to be pointed. This city embraces its team, in the very fabric of daily living. A glimpse of what this team means to the people of Philadelphia was shown to the world when circa 2million people collected on a single four mile stretch to celebrate and join cheering the Phillies on the post World Series parade. All cities create a parade and celebrate home town victors but there has never been a pouring of emotion for a team, perhaps challenged by the 1969 Miracle Mets.

Philadelphia is a city that lives, sleeps and breaths its Phillies, Eagles, Flyers, and 76ers. Middle of the night revelers' favorite song is Fly Eagles Fly, and in September the city was all about the Phillies.

The one constant that I noticed about the every-day meaning of the sports teams to the city of Philadelphia is conversation.

I travel to every major city in the country regularly, and I have been to every MLB stadium. In every city I go, I ask the same questions; to the cab drivers, hotel desks, business partners, restaurant customers and employees, people in the elevators and pretty much anyone, "how's it going?" "How's your day going?" I always talk to my friends about how I am amazed that everyone responds in terms of their jobs. Tips are down, business is this or that, boss is this or that, etc. but it is always about the job.

Except in Philadelphia; all summer the reply was always about the Phillies and or Eagles. The Phillies are on a roll, the Eagles this or that. It seemed that the city psyche zeroed in on sports instead of the job. The ownership had invested in the team, the team responded and it all culminated in a 2million person parade. It was truly amazing. The ownership seems completely connected into this energy and Philadelphia is an exciting town to be for a sports fan.

Recap; the Mets are much stronger on paper than they were the previous two years, the Braves are developing a new team and the Marlins will be competitive but the Phillies total organization seems to be working, even after it won the World Series, on all "Ticker" cylinders with all ships sailing in the same direction.

The team is balanced in offense, defense, pitching, and in terms of veterans to youth, and the ownership moved from investing circa $89million to $98million last year to $132million to offset the Mets investments. Just keep an eye on alternative pitching options in order to keep this momentum.

(Note to Phillies and Mets: the Marlins believe they have the pitching and offense to rain on your parades and take the division and leave the others to battle for the Wild Card. This is the whisper team).

PHILLIES SCORE CARD			
Criteria	**RYG**	**success 1L-20 H**	**elevator speech**
Owner Maximizers	Green	17	Past conservative Profit Maximizers who loosened up last year as I called for! Looks like they got it and won the WS. Improved more in 2009. Passionate city excited
Owner Contract risk	Yellow	15	Derivative risk averse but now a plus in deep recession. Weakness became strength. Team increased budge 10%+ as I called for. Got Hamel and Howard signed. Still wish they got 1 more pitcher
Transaction Philosophy:			
Buy low, sell high	Yellow	16	Without a WS victory the team model doubted for falling short. Victory the ultimate defense; Working model of build from within, strong scouting, free agent missing pieces now influence other teams.
Value draft picks vs. free agents	Green	17	Values its minors and scouting use of draft picks over risky free agents. When pull the trigger it's from budget driven weakness.
Improve through player changes	Yellow	16	Pitching a continual struggle due to supply/demand in inflexible budget range.
Stock of rare skilled players	Green	17	Farm team producing World Class talent in post steroid, in recession economy.
Forget pocket cost	Green	17	Abreu moved to change team chemistry. Thome strong but made move for Howard.
Adjust to division and league	Green	18	Head to head the past two years, when the chips were down the Phils clobbered the Mets. Division got stronger. Outspent by Mets, Phils will be challenged again.
Don't be Yankees farm system	Yellow	15	Much improved. Amazing what a difference 1 year makes.
Trade through strength	Yellow	14	Conservative, limited risk, budget limits the team but wise trades and respect now a positive to team set minus 1 more pitcher.
Balance of needs with budget	Yellow	16	Erased 2 player short stigma, positioned for future in weak economy. Wish they signed 1 more pitcher. Age of Moyer could be the snake in the grass this season.
General Management	Green	17	Gillick still in background. Amaro long time part of long time system philosophy.
Scouting	Green	17	Consistent strategy and discipline. Farm system proving World Class production.
Field Management	Green	17	Manager cool-calm proved to be World Champion attribute. Players responded.

Paul Martino

Section 2

Performance Enhancements

Chapter 4

The Hypocrisy of Policing Performance

I propose that illegal steroids remain illegal and MLB banned because they kill and the innocent players need to be protected from having to compete with players using these illegal substances. MLB should simplify its performance policing to this manageable criteria. If substances are USA Federal legal then MLB should not ban them. The chapters in this section will explain the policing, testing, adherence, science and medical, ethical, and manageability reasons for this position. Minus this proposal, this section will provide insight into the coming repercussions.

I found over the past few years that there is understandable confusion, misconception and ambiguity of what makes any substance "performance enhancement." I address this dilemma in terms of relevance to sports competition and progress in past, current and future terms. I will cover in the following chapter the impact of performance enhancement drugs on General Management decision making.

I don't profess to be right; I just want to get it right. I will provide my observations and let you determine what you think. Take your beliefs and views to the mlb.com blogs and blogs across the internet. Get the debate to the airwaves and tabloids.

Assumption 1:

The generally understood definition of competitive sports "performance enhancement substance" in society today is the intake by pill, liquid, cream or inhalation of a substance that may provide an unequal advantage over the competition in either direct competition or over time.

Assumption 2:

The "real world" application for the definition of competitive sports "performance enhancement substance" by baseball governing body and society today is the intake by pill, liquid, cream or inhalation of an unapproved and/or illegal substance that may provide an unequal advantage over the competition in direct competition.

Assumption 3:

Whether or not the competitive sports "performance enhancement substance" is safe by medical standards does not appear to me to be the official driving determination for the acceptance or banishment of the substance(s). There is no hard evidence that the list of banned substances is uniquely different than other substances approved or at least not banned.

In addition, "performance enhancement substance" does not address external performance enhancers such muscle transplants (i.e. Tommy John surgery). Artificial limbs and future muscle "robotics" and other physical performance changers are not considered in the definition. As well, external physical attachments (i.e. the shoe used by the Philadelphia Eagles field goal kicker, Tom Dempsey and then banned by the NFL) are considered a component of approved equipment and other definitions.

Assumption 4:

Generally, people think of "banned" as bad, bad means it is not good and/or unfair, using the banned is unethical and/or illegal, if you use the banned then you are bad; if you are bad, you must pay your debt to society for your badness; Pretty logical and acceptable thinking for the collective society.

Assumption 5:

The prohibited substances defined and identified in section 2B of the May 23, 2008 revised Major League Baseball Joint Prevention and Treatment Program Basic Agreement, publicly provided for download at http://mlbplayers.mlb.com/pa/info/cba.jsp is in-scope discussion in this chapter. Sections 2A (Drugs of Abuse), 2C (Stimulants) and 2D (Adding Prohibiting Substances) are out of scope for this book.

In addition, all other sections regarding the Oversight and Administration, Selection and Tenure, Testing (except for section 3G), Evaluation and Treatment, Follow-Up Testing, Confidentiality, Disclosure of Information, Discipline, Appeals, Education, Cost of Program, Rights of Third Parties, and Term; all identified in the MLB Joint Prevention and Treatment Program document are out of scope for this discussion.

Section 3G is the (Therapeutic Use Exemption) section of May 23, 2008 revised Major League Baseball Joint Prevention and Treatment Program Basic Agreement, publicly provided for download at http://mlbplayers.mlb.com/pa/info/cba.jsp is included because some banned substances are permitted under defined criteria such as doctor oversight.

Overview

I break down competitive sports "performance enhanced substance" in this chapter into five observations, and one proposal:

1. Anabolic and androgenic steroids observation
2. Cortisone observation
3. HGH observation
4. The Real Story – Performance enhancement vs. steroids (some)
5. Other substances
6. Proposal

This Chapter overview of observations is that Major League Baseball (MLB) focus on performance enhancement substances is important, is making positive strides but on a macro level, the understanding and focus is turned upside down. Focus should be:

Performance Enhancement Substances			
All Steroids			

(Where steroids is a subset of the overall performance substance focus)

Focus is currently:

```
┌─────────────────────────────────────────┐
│             Illegal Steroids            │
│                                          │
│   Performance                            │
│   Enhancement                            │
│   Substances                             │
│                                          │
└─────────────────────────────────────────┘
```

(Where performance enhancement substances is a subset of the overall steroid focus)

I break down the greater performance enhancement issue into both public and athletic categories and the medical profession role:

	legal over the counter & MLB OK	legal but not MLB OK	illegal under all conditions	In use but not focus of USA or MLB	Considered safe or unknown	Considered dangerous	1 low-10 high ease physician obtain	Used by athletes and public	Suspected use by Actors and similar	Who's winning -masker/policers	Elevator Points
Cortisone & prednisone			X		X		1	X		NA	- Not applicable. No focus of banned substances - A steroid for use to mask pain vs. heal body - Signifiant harm to body with greater use
HGH & testosterone		X			X		6	X	X	P	- MLB ok if proven body HGH level was too low - Muscle growth healing attribute. Body naturally produces - Unknown long term use impact. Not designer drug
Designer / Analbolic steroids			X				10		X	P	- Illegal and banned. Should not be used by anyone - History of shortened athletes lives after long term use - These steroids greatest harm on MLB
Other "GNC" & non-USA avail	X	X	X				1	X	X	NA	- some items only available in Asia, carribean - many GNC items banned by MLB. Some not defined - mix of legal items can produce HGH results
B12				X			1			NA	- no better than Redbull - 5hr drinks similar - not typically given by physicians any longer
Newly created mask agents		X	X				10			M	- Richer athletes access to items not known by policers - These kept secret so can avoid banned use discovery - Policers reactive over long term

Observation 1: Anabolic and androgenic steroids

The rules and law are clear specifically regarding anabolic and androgenic steroids. Sections 2, Section 2B(Performance Enhancement Substances), and 3G (Therapeutic Use Exemption) of the May 23, 2008 revised Major League Baseball Joint Prevention and Treatment Program Basic Agreement states the illegal use. The reading is a bit dry so those who want to see the specific wording can go to http://mlbplayers.mlb.com/pa/info/cba.jsp in order to review.

I agree that the drugs classified as illegal should be banned because there is ample evidence over time, across sports about their destructive impact. Athletes have testified to the damage these have done to them. Steroids can be deadly over the long term and short term effects are significant. These effects are well documented throughout medical journals, the internet, in books, and in testimonies. Innocent players should be protected from having to take these destructive substances in order to compete and make an honest living.

If illegal use of steroids under US Federal law were permitted for any players to be used recreationally or unsupervised, other players would be forced to take these steroids in order to keep up. This scenario would put the health and life at risk for the entire player fraternity. For this reason I fully support the laws and banishment of these substances.

From a personal perspective I gave up putting sugar on my Wheaties after I read the book, "Sugar Blues." I never smoked a cigarette after elementary school showed us a healthy clean, pink lung and then a crispy charcoaled lung of a smoker. Steroid use was certainly never appealing to me. I did compete (tried) against some obvious steroid users and it was not fun.

Observation 2A: Use of Cortisone

Thurman Munson is my favorite baseball player of all time. He knew the game, studied the game, and played every play like it was his last play in his career. He was a clutch hitter.

Thurman Munson competed with "The Ticker."

Thurman Munson was the classic player who brought the competitive intangibles advantage that leads teams to be Champions, the intangibles that do not show up in the statistics. In fact, Thurman Munson is the poster example of what my books profess; live and compete in life with a competitive anger, a ticker that only gets stronger when the going gets toughest.

Thurman Munson was a leader who played the game honestly, cleanly, by the rules, and led by example. Thurman Munson even played an influential role in getting Reggie Jackson, who he famously struggled with from a personality perspective, moved into his rightful power slot in the lineup; a tactical move that helped trigger the Yankees winning stretch that led the team over the Red Sox, and on to World Champions.

This leader, Thurman Munson, was also the toughest player of his day. He was the tough guy's tough guy. Mr. Tough Guy. "The Captain" refused to acknowledge pain and injury. As a catcher he would take fouls off of his legs and arms and home plate "bull run" collision hits from charging base runners that would have other players rolling on the ground. Other players would allow the trainer to come out and rub the pain away and spray their body with numbing spray so they could keep playing.

Not Thurman.

He'd put on his scowl, curse under his breath, walk around a bit and tell the trainer to get away from him. He would not rub or acknowledge the pain himself either. He was a football player's baseball player, a hockey player's baseball player.

I still have the **April 1978 "Sport" magazine, *"Sparky & Goose"* article by Harry Stein, page 78** passage where Goose Gossage and Spark Lyle talked about Thurman Munson. (Direct passage):

"One guy I'll be glad to have on my side is [Yankee catcher] Thurman Munson," says Gossage. "Christ, he's tough. I once got him square on the arm with a 100-mph fastball and he just grinned. Later, in the clubhouse, I got a note from him. 'I took your best f---ing shot, you cockroach. (Signed) The White Gorilla'" (End passage).

In business, I always refer to sports for examples and guidance. I still regularly think back to what Thurman Munson represented before I go into a tough negotiation or dealing with tough conflict. Yes, I want to earn the respect for how I approach business preparation, teamwork, and for a high level of ethics standard, but I equally want to earn respect leading with Thurman Munson competitive anger, "Ticker."

Now as a young fan I remember announcers talking on TV during games about Thurman Munson being so banged up over the course of the year that he needed to be given a cortisone shot in order to step back out on the field the next game. Thurman, like many players, needed the shot or else he could not compete.

Cortisone was ok because a player with severe pain and injuries too unbearable to deal with on the playing field could play after receiving a cortisone shot.

Since the 1970s, the number of players who took cortisone shots in order to play the game is in the THOUSANDS, maybe tens of thousands. Thousands of players have taken cortisone shots multiple times over the course of a season. Players take cortisone shots today.

Cortisone, it can be argued, is as part of baseball fabric as the designated hitter. I choose designated hitter as an example because some consider the DH as a necessary evil, others believe it should be banned, and today one league has it while the other does without.

Openly many stars have needed cortisone shots to finish the season and to play in the post season; all of these players are taking cortisone shots in order to enhance their performance and to even perform AT ALL. Many great performances came with the help of cortisone.

Ok, a player is hurt; he goes to the doctor, who makes him able to tolerate pain and play, possibly even delay a much needed operation until after the season. He gives the player a cortisone shot.

Cortisone is no walk in the park. The body goes through significant adjustments for days in order to adapt to the shot itself. The player can only receive so many shots over the course of the year and within a certain time frame or the body will react harshly. If the player reaches the maximum number of injections and still can't play then he's out of luck; he's on the DL and is not going to play. Even if there is a doctor who will give him the shot, the body is not going to cooperate.

The Mayo Clinic provides insight into the realities of cortisone at: http://www.mayoclinic.com/health/cortisone-shots/MY00268

Essentially cortisone, based upon review of all major public publications, is often used for arthritis and other aging factor pains, as well as arthritis and many other sport related injuries and limitations.

Getting a cortisone shot is not like going to the doctor for a flu shot. Pitchers even need to get cortisone shots days in advance of pitching or they will be unable to pitch.

Cortisone is a steroid.

Observation 2B: Variations of Cortisone

Cortisone is a steroid.

The American Heritage Dictionary definition of cortisone, provided by Yahoo Education provides a 20K foot definition.

I found no directly defined matches for corticosterone, corticosteroid and $C_{21}H_{28}O_5$ in the banned substance list in the Basic Agreement you can download at http://mlbplayers.mlb.com/pa/info/cba.jsp .

Section 3G (Therapeutic Use Exemption) of the Basic Agreement provides medical exceptions to banned substances but Cortisone is not listed as a banned substance. What interests me is that Cortisone can technically be used to address adrenal insufficiency, arthritis, and other aging factor pains. To me that means improvement of endurance, to improve performance. "Allergies" is a red flag to me also.

The www.Answers.com/topic/cortisone definition of cortisone provides a more granular list of definitions, giving us a 1K foot definition including references to food, fitness and dental uses.

None of the terms (i.e. *17hydroxy-11-dehydrocorticosterone*) are directly identified in the Basic Agreement.

I confirmed with the medical community that cortisone is a generally used substance today. There are increased methods of applying cortisone today. Essentially there is a strong likelihood that players on your favorite team needed to apply cortisone today while you read this book.

You can read all of the additional details and definitions at www.Answers.com/topic/cortisone but I want to focus on what peaks my interest and raises red flags to me in terms of both baseball related performance enhancement and safety to the individual (I include safety because that is the prime reason why anabolic steroids are banned). What blurs the black and white lines on what is a performance enhancer between the playing field lines:

1. Cortisone is also available as **Cortisone Acetate Oral tablet.**
2. The list of risks, cautions, dangerous mixes with other drugs, foods, conditions, etc. is shocking. As with many other steroids and other banned substances, the harm due to misuse is substantial.

Cortisone is legal and, as a long precedent, is approved to be used in Major League Baseball.

Cortisone is a steroid.

Observation 3: HGH

Andy Pettitte acknowledged in 2007 to the public that he regretfully took what became a banned "performance enhancing substance" in 2006; his use was on a few occasions, and stopped by 2005. Andy Pettitte took HGH (Human Growth Hormone).

Andy, if I understand his public acknowledgment and apology correctly, indicated that he only took HGH when he was injured. He only took HGH when he was injured because it reduced the number of months it took for his body to heal from his injuries. When he was healthy, he stopped taking HGH because he didn't need it; he stopped when his body had healed.

HGH takes on the attributes of the body's pituitary glands, and helps athletes recover from injuries and stress. Essentially it helps cell reproduction. The extreme advertisements claim that it delays the aging process. More mainstream medical application is to increase an individual's energy level, the stamina, and improve bone density. Essentially it has anabolic characteristics.

One of countless reference sites on HGH is:
http://en.wikipedia.org/wiki/Growth_hormone_treatment

If Andy Pettitte had not taken HGH, he would have lost additional months in playing time. The team would have paid more of the $millions to Andy without the performance.

Andy is one of many players who are suspected or admitted to using HGH.

Outside the baseball lines, in society, HGH is prescribed by doctors to some men in their 50s and 60s in order to enable them to have the strength and stamina to exercise. My focus here is the facts; HGH heals injured athletes more quickly than minus HGH, and doctors provide HGH to older men in order for them to function and perform normally.

Not clear about Andy Pettitte's confession, as well as many of the other players being called out:

- Why he didn't just go to a doctor like everyone else in society? If he was injured this could be approved.

- Why players feel the need to go into the back rooms of society and lie about using HGH. HGH is legal.

- The MLB Joint Drug Agreement went into effect in 2006. Before then, HGH was not a banned substance. In addition, even with the implementation of the collective bargaining agreement ban of HGH in 2006, there is a section 3G of the Joint Drug Agreement (see http://mlbplayers.mlb.com/pa/info/cba.jsp) that approves medical oversight use of substances. Still the players hid and lied.

- There is public stigma of taking HGH but cortisone is normal course of business. Players hide the use of something that is no worse to healing or playing through injuries than cortisone?

I'm not connecting the dots. There is a greater story here that has not yet been uncovered.

The Real Story of Performance Enhancement vs. Steroids (some) Why is cortisone approved and accepted but HGH is banned and players ostracized?

I unscientifically sampled 100 fans across the country during an 8 month time frame in 2008; each of these persons had expressed outrage about players who took banned substances. I surveyed:

- "Is HGH a steroid?" 82% said, "I'm not sure."
- "Is HGH illegal?" "66% said, "Yes."

I don't believe we the Public understand what is happening with sports related "performance enhancing substances."

Every fan has an opinion about the use of certain "performance enhancing substances," (steroids) and what they have done to baseball and sports in general. Everyone has an opinion about the legalities of certain "performance enhancing substance" (steroids), cheating, ethical behavior, the players' rights to secrecy, the government cases against players who lied under oath and everyone has opinions about the impact of certain "performance enhancing substances" (steroids) on sports and sports records. We all generally agree that illegal steroids are, in most circumstances, bad. The fact that they are illegal is simple enough to ban from baseball. It is illegal so it is banned. I can connect those dots.

My concern is with the source of what is driving all of these public issues, debates, lawsuits, prosecutions and banishments about the greater subject of "performance enhancement substances." I argue that all fragmented aspects of performance progress have been bundled into the topic of illegal steroids.

This perceived greater misconception is the seed that builds the greater issue regarding deciding what are the "good" vs. "bad" performance enhancers, who is making these binding decisions, how does time change the approval or banning of the "good" and the "bad" sources, and ultimately, does it all have to be so complicated? Does baseball need to be Olympics level restrictive on performance enhancers? In this age where medicine and science fiction is surpassing current day realities, is it possible to control what no one seems to understand?

So, why is cortisone approved and accepted but HGH is banned and players ostracized?

Recently it has become public knowledge that some players have:
- Both used illegal steroids and HGH
- Used both HGH and cortisone
- Used only HGH.

All of the players in these cases used the now banned substance, HGH. There are hundreds of past and current players, known and suspected to have taken at least illegal steroids. Why are fans, management, and players so outraged at the use of HGH? Why is Andy Pettitte an outcast to some, why is his career blemished, why did he need to apologize to other players who openly took shots of cortisone in order to play the game of baseball?

On the flip side, are the players we forgave because they only used HGH for injuries, like Andy Pettitte, holding back on a greater story for some reason about their use? Is it the stigma? Why is there a stigma if it is no worse than cortisone?

From a 30k foot point of view my question is not that important. Simply don't take a banned substance and you don't face Assumption 4 that I list at the beginning of this chapter. Laws are laws, rules are rules, follow them, right?

Well, not all rules and laws are just or logical. There were laws at one time that kept blacks and women from voting. Blindly accepting laws and rules without question, in my opinion, is just as wrong as the unjust laws and rules. I believe there should be more informed debate regarding HGH specifically, and then steroids (both legal and illegal) vs. targeted "performance enhancement substances" in general.

Maybe, like the designated hitter rule, once people understand exactly what the issue is, some will be in better position to make quantifiable judgment calls for it emphatically, and others will be just as strongly against it, others won't care. Maybe the rules will be changed. Maybe players will be able to play into their mid 50s. At least the debate will not be bundled as a subset of illegal steroids (cortisone is a steroid).

Right now the only view is that someone took a banned substance. Everyone is outraged. The player is permanently marked. Where is the debate on the specifically banned substances? Why are we just accepting that long list of long medical terms in the Joint Prevention and Treatment document that we know are often available at GNC?

Maybe everything stays on the list. Ok. Fine, but why don't we know after all of these years of debate? What products are not available at GNC but are over the counter in Latin American countries or Asia? This is as great a black mark, in my opinion, on our public media as it is on the baseball establishment and players. Is our news so sanitized now that it is too easy to call a player out as guilty instead of detailing what makes what he specifically did so detrimental to the game?

The cases against many players including; Bonds, Clemens, Rodriguez, McGwire, Sosa, Palmeiro, and others is clear. If they did illegal steroids then they should be kept out of the Hall of Fame. If they lied, the government will determine if they go to jail.

We need to separate the greater performance enhancement debate from the steroid issue instead of bundling everything under the steroid umbrellas as public understanding has evolved.

When I was a teenager the drinking age was 21 but so many 18 year old kids were dying in Vietnam that, because it didn't seem reasonable to send our kids to war but not let them have a beer, they lowered the drinking age to 18. After many years of teenagers being killed in alcohol related deaths, many states raised the drinking age back to 21. Some countries don't have drinking age laws. Whatever the reasons and decisions pro or con, I'm fine with the fact that there are quantifiable reasons, factual debates driving these decisions. In the case of HGH, I don't believe we the People, and the baseball Lords, collectively have control of the facts that are driving the decisions.

Insiders indicate that players can combine legal substances at GNC that perform as well as HGH without it showing up as HGH. Do we the Public or the Lords of Baseball have any clue what is going on here? We've got great villains and headlines and no clue.

It is not just HGH. Evidence indicates that most baseball related people and fans have a limited, associative level of understanding of what many other items on the banned list actually do or don't do vs. similar substances that are perfectly fine. Passion and general opinion are outweighing some of the facts about the difference between steroids specifically and performance enhancements as a whole.

Observation 4: Other substances

Minus the harmful and illegal steroids; performance enhancement, for lack of a better term, is GOOD.

I think about players' physical preparation for competition in the 1970s, before weight training; lifting weights was considered a career ending move because it would diminish a player's natural "baseball skills." Baseball was a game not for athletes but for God given naturally skilled players; players who were born with the ability to through 90mph, hit 40 homeruns, steal 50 bases, and hit .300. Natural ability, not training and nutritional regimens were the creation of baseball players.

I remember debates we fans had when it seemed evident that Carlton Fisk was lifting weights in the early 1980s. He was definitely the exception, and some wondered if the weight lifting hurt his swing and ended his career early. That was the mantra for the first 100 years of baseball; don't lift weights. Baseball skills are natural skills. Weights will make you bulky, inflexible and unable to play the game. Back then loading up on lots of carbohydrates was good, protein not so good. Vitamins were still a novelty. There was only one kind of weight lifting; body builder-like weight lifting. As a fan, I think of the Yankees Ron Bloomberg when I think of the early 1970s as a reason not to lift weights. Weight lifting was "bad."

Nolan Ryan is the first player I can remember who focused on cycling to keep the legs strong. Interestingly, I don't remember any players lifting weights and working out until aside from Carlton Fisk until… Jose Canseco...

From what we know today, any player who would have reduced the carbohydrates, lifted repetitive weights, and took more vitamins in the 1970s would have had a competitive advantage over the course of the season, especially during the "dog days of August."

Pitchers had the advantage over hitters in the spring but many would wear down in that summer heat and their endurance would diminish toward the end of the season (still some truth to this today but nutrition, travel improvements, vitamins and exercise plans lessen this edge today – performance enhancing improvements).

Imagine being able to take the currently legal, approved food and training options athletes have today and being able to give them to just a few players. What an advantage! Would Hall-of-Famers Tom Seaver and Steve Carlton been able to pitch another 5-10 years at the top of their games? Would it have given Willie Mays another 5 productive years? To dream, to dream!

When Nolan Ryan retired, he could still strike out 10 batters per game, potentially throw another no-hitter, and throw 90-100mph. It was the injuries that set in to a man edging closer to 50 than 40 that had the Hall-of-Fame giant retire. Could some "cutting edge" medically supervised program have given him another 5-10 years? To dream, to dream!

The players who were on the cutting edge of physical training twenty years ago, minus steroids, helped trend players to now excel into their 40s. Previously, players would begin to move into pasture as early as their early to mid 30s. Players who lasted to their 40s often had long past great or even respectable seasons. Nolan Ryan and others raised performance and retirement bars through the legal and approved means we accept as normal today.

Just to plant the seed of doubt in what we assume about player banning legal "performance enhancement," what about Lasyk? There are players who can play an additional 5-10 years because of Lasyk, which is not banned. Some of these same players can get regular steroid (cortisone) shots. So, why is there a stigma around medically prescribed HGH? From a power perspective, it was MLB that allowed better bats, tighter baseballs, and smaller stadiums all to influence more homeruns. These are statistical power enhancers.

Should risk be a substance ban criteria? There is certainly risk and bodily damage involved with cortisone shots. Also, a small percentage of people lose their eye sight or their sight gets worse from Lasyk surgery. Does permitting Lasyk put ballplayers at greater risk than cortisone? Does one player getting Lasyk force a competing teammate to risk his eyesight by getting Lasyk in order to enhance his performance? Studies show that some persons who get Lasyk surgery can see even better than 20/20. This would provide a player with a competitive performance advantage he would not otherwise have.

What if they come out with a Lasyk that is so good that a batter can easily see each seam on the pitcher thrown ball? If he can tell the ball is a curve ball or a fast ball and his average increases by 75 percentage points, does every other player have to go out and get Lasyk? Will Lasyk then be banned for players with 20/20 vision? What if these players can then play until they are 60? Science is getting a lot better in these areas. A story this off-season discussed "artificial eyesight." It's arriving for the blind. Where will it be in 20 years?

What about coffee, green tea and other herbs? What about all of these other drugs that doctors subscribe today. Admittedly, I don't know what most of the terms are that are being sold on television today. Are any of these providing an edge on ball players greater than HGH? What about Viagra? Can main street folks be allowed to take performance enhancers but pro athletes legally be held back in order to keep their careers? Why can a baseball player take some of the substances sold at any GNC while other substances at GNC will get him banned from baseball? I am not connecting the dots here on how we got good vs. bad, MLB banned vs. ok, <u>so complicated.</u>

I am not willing to blindly embrace Assumption 4 at the top of the chapter based upon blindly accepting Assumption 2; what specifically are we outraged about?

What about moving forward? Will it turn out that medically supervised substance "XYZ" in labs today, secretly out in the next generation of player blood stream tomorrow make Joba Chamberlain be to pitch to 60? What legal stand will MLB have to stop him if it is not illegal? <u>You cannot keep a person from aging because he is an MLB member, while the rest of society is permitted to improve its health.</u>

MLB wants this "problem" to go away at the dawn of physical and mental science and medical breakthroughs. The Steroid Era – Performance Enhancement Era has only just begun.

Major League Baseball is reactionary and not prepared. Based upon ambiguous reference to "banned" the public seems ready to convict without knowing why or that "banned" does not mean "illegal." At the same time players are making their own situation worse by lying about their usage. [Once a player lies, the entire game is changed].

Observation 5: Manageable Policing and Masking

I repeatedly state that I don't profess to be right but I want us all to get it right; you, me, MLB management, the Union, and players. Realistic and manageable oversight of performance enhancement substances needs to be a top priority for MLB; MLB needs to understand the performance boundaries it is able to manage and then set policing guidelines in step with the laws of the United States.

Going beyond this fundamental discipline will continue to be unmanageable, cause the game great pain, and move the burden of player health and legality responsibility of the United States onto the mutual shoulders of MLB management and the MLBPA Union. History shows that the overall well-being is a mutual concern for both the Union and MLB but each entity has competing priorities related to the rights and privileges of the individual members. MLB is not in position to manage all known and ongoing legal substances. It is simply not viable.

Policing and compliance has gotten so complicated that players have to purchase vitamins and other products from MLB sponsored vendors just to be sure that there is not some arbitrary, ambiguous, negligible substance in a product legally purchased over the counter. This is not the amateur Olympics, every four years. This is an 8 month season, 1 month pre-season, and 3 months of training culture every year.

Let's be street smart; there are very rare, expensive masking agents available today for legal but MLB banned substances that star players are taking. Follow the money; a player pays $2million for a masking agent and makes $25million in performance edge over his pears. Save your outrage for my statement for someone with blinders on.

The maskers will stay ahead of the policers. Some masking agents will be uncovered and MLB will be going through this same sad story all over again.

We do know that designer and anabolic steroids are illegal and the policers are all over any attempts at masking cheating. We can manage the policing of illegal steroids and we have the backing of the Federal government. The chemical breakdown and masking agents are well known and policing is strong. These cheaters should go down.

All other illegal substances are relatively police-able, and even if difficult to police, there should be strong enough stigma and legal consequence that the players will avoid their use. When it comes to every-day performance enhancers MLB has set itself up to fail.

Regarding both masking agents and new legal performance enhancers, MLB will always be in reactive mode. The rich player will find ways to obtain the substances and maintain an artificial advantage over the other players.

Today the outrage is HGH, tomorrow someone will find something new that the top players may be taking. The media will be outraged and players will step to the podium, crying, and saying I'm sorry I took this substance that wasn't banned at the time…blah, blah.

The current day players caught for HGH and over the counter substances, but not illegal substances, lost a great opportunity to provide public awareness and to open the public court of opinion. These players did a great disservice to the players today who know that additional unpublicized cheating is going on but cannot prove it or want to attach their name to the debate.

I wish these players had higher ethical standards, and had not taken any banned substances. I wish MLB players would have fought for certain substances and ground rules instead of hiding in back alleys, lying, and covering up their actions. If they were guilty of using only banned substances but nothing illegal, then A-Rod, Clemens, Pettitte and the others should have gone to the podium and said;

"You got me. I knowingly took HGH because it saved injury recovery time by months, it gave me endurance in August, and when I took it I knew it was legal. I disagreed with baseball then and I do now. I stand by my use. I knew what I was doing then so I can't say sorry for getting caught.

You got me, so do what you want with me. Keep me out of the Hall of Fame, wipe away my records, or even put my picture up on an "MLB not allowed" wall or anything you want. At the end of the day I don't agree with your ban, it wasn't banned at the time I used it, and I am not sorry.

You got me, I got tired of drinking red bull, getting cortisone to hide the injury instead of healing it quickly, I got tired of drinking pots of coffee for caffeine before games and I did it. Change the rules because they are not fair and I'm not sorry."

I would have respected that honest stance. That would have been acceptable. Maybe we would still ban the players. Maybe public opinion and outcry would remain the same.

At least the public would have taken a closer look at what is being banned. The public would have understood the difference between illegal steroids and other performance enhancements. If the public still was outraged, then ok. But these players, by skewing the truth, simply apologizing, and giving sad excuses for why they were bad boys brings no earned respect.

At the end of the day, MLB should be more street smart in laying down governance that is manageable (simpler), realistic, and lock step with Federal US law. Beyond that basic premise, the league that wants to "put this all behind us" sets itself up to fail with ongoing loss of credibility for a very long time.

This issue has been developing beyond this past year, the past decade. This didn't begin in the 1990s and likely not in the 1980s. This issue has been developing for 30-40 years with the same mistakes over and over repeatedly.

I am taking a rational stance from a realistic manageability perspective, aligned with US Federal Law. It is my stance that any more complicated and we the Public will be shaming players in another 30-40 years.

For the sake of the game, for the sake of player statistics, let's get the debates about the game back to player on-field performance comparisons, baseball era by era; let's simplify policing and get the debate out of the laboratories. Let's add legal performance to the different baseball eras comparisons of bat and ball quality, stadium sizes, and other comparisons that make this game great. Let's leave the illegal issues to the government and police.

Policing Proposal

Illegal and damaging use of steroids in baseball must be permanently cleaned up. Players who break this code need to be punished and must be held accountable for their actions. Those who extend their actions by deceiving the fans, their teams, and the government need to pay the maximum penalties. That process is a work in progress today.

What I propose is a separate, greater focus on performance enhancement substances. Currently it seems that the blind baseball justice pendulum may have swayed too much toward the executioners becoming blind.

A person can drown just as easily when they are 1 inch under water as they are when they are 10 feet submerged. Before I condemn any player, like Andy Pettitte, for any specific substance I want to know exactly what it is that substance is and how it relates to other approved substances. I want to know how many players in 2003 and after only passed tests because they had advance notice. I want the list of who was tipped off. I want the 104 names now that A-Rod was thrown under the bus by one of the supposedly ethical "policers."

I cannot say the lines are clear against HGH vs. for cortisone and other "performance enhancers." I won't be outraged about a topic we know 10 inches about when the facts are 10 feet high. A review of performance enhancements need to be the focus with steroids as a component of the review, not performance enhancements as a component of steroids, which I believe is the case today. Performance enhancement issues include smaller ballparks, tighter baseballs, better bats, and even who, knew what and when. How many players only passed their tests because they knew in advance that they were going to be tested and had time to go clean?

At the end of the day, I believe baseball should keep it simple; if it is legal then it is ok. No stigma for using any legal performance enhancer or injury recovery substance. Baseball should live by these four basic laws:

1. If it is illegal then it is banned. This includes Major League Baseball Joint Prevention and Treatment Program Basic Agreement:
   a. Drugs of abuse listed in section 2A. These include all listed and Sections I and II of the Code of Federal Regulations.
   b. Performance enhancement substances currently both listed in section 2B and are illegal in the USA Section III of the Code of Federal Regulations.
   c. Stimulants currently both listed in section 2C and are illegal in the USA according to Section III of the Code of Federal Regulations.
   d. Ongoing additions of prohibited substances to the program listed in section 2D and additions to Sections I, II and/or III.
2. If it is not illegal then it is not banned. Keep it traceable, manageable, and aligned with the fabric and laws of our society. Special governance at the Olympic level is not viable for our sport that is 8 months a year vs. once every four years.
3. If it is illegal but there is solid proof that it should not be illegal, then go to Washington, lobby for change, and get it reversed and then make it approved.
4. If a player uses any illegal substance, then they are banned from the game.
5. There is always an *asterisk. Proven masking agents specifically designed to hide illegal use, with no other attribute need to remain banned.

Chapter 5

Cheating Impact from Wall Street to Ballpark Way

Red Flags – Statistics on Steroids

If you equate my Wall Street decisions this past off-season with a General Manager of a Major League baseball team, you would be calling for my head on a paper plate platter. Yes, fans would be flooding the airways for my firing, newspapers would be on fire about the demise of the team, and we would be set for a last place finish. After so many years of getting it text-book right, I got it so wrong. What did I do so wrong?

I focused on energy stocks that had recently peaked on news that the global economy would drive sustained higher demand for the diminishing supply. Our economy had hit a rough patch; energy stocks dipped from all time highs to lows not seen in not only the past year, but in the past 5 years! This was a classic buying opportunity. Warren Buffet was jumping in with circa $10billion! Green flag! If I understood correctly, Boone Pickens believed that oil would never drop below $58 a barrel and here we were at the bottom of expectations! Green light! I checked with industry subject matter experts (the MLB scouts, long time GMs and All-Stars of the energy industries); they felt it was a great buy situation.

The laws of supply and demand were in classic position with buy lowEST, sell highEST. There are hedging stocks you can invest in for energy in case energy stocks decline instead of increase but these stocks were at 5-10 year lows so I didn't balance the risk. I was petal to the metal going for that once in a decade or longer opportunity. I am frugal, a fiscal conservative but this was the text book opportunity that you wait for.

In baseball terms I had this great team that was poised to be in the playoffs and make a World Championship run. Suddenly Giambi, Clemens, Knoblauch, McGwire and Rodriguez all became free agents and they all wanted to join my team – for the MLB minimum. This, to me, was like the Yankees getting Babe Ruth. What happened?

We now know that the market was artificially high, on a deck of cards due to financial leaders, like $millionaire ballplayers on steroids, not playing by the rules. Banks figured out how to make one bad loan turn into fifteen so they could make bigger bonus checks. The situation ultimately got so bad that it led to the unprecedented, historic crash and burn collapse of entire USA and global financial structures within one year. This led to the cliff dive drop in energy demand, increase in supply and the investment mechanisms adjusted to a calibrated equilibrium.

In hard terms, what I determined was the lowest of lows dropped an additional 75% based upon trending and forecasting data we now know was obsolete and tainted.

I disregarded the red flags, blinded by the green flags. I should have been more street smart and less book smart. Like the MLB GM signing the player with great stats but unknowingly on steroids, I dropped my guard, didn't diversify to balance the risk and let myself get burned. I imagine these stocks will rebound and it's fine over time. However, the General Manager doesn't have five years to get it right.

White Flags – The GM Steroid Dilemma

Major League Baseball General Managers, whose careers and fan wrath lay with each and every move, make decisions based upon very specific assumptions; player statistics, health, character, projection of future growth, projections, trending, and chemistry (team chemistry-not steroid chemistry). When regression data is tainted then the GM is better off throwing away the stats and making all decisions by getting out of the swivel chair and making decisions on scouting and SME observations of players.

A General Manager may pay a superstar in upwards of 10-20% of the team payroll. Stars get $10-25million to be the cornerstone of team success based upon their previous statistics, training program and health. Steroids throw those stats out the window.

The General Manager plays by ethical rules based upon Major League Baseball Law and USA Law. The rules are as clear as the rules between the playing field lines. The assumption used to be that players collectively do not cheat. Over time there was suspicion, and many players are still just under suspicion, but there now are Federal, Mitchell and "whisper" lists with a lot of names; the evidence is mounts on the guilt side of the scale.

I had many debates in the 1990s with my father, a baseball purist who grew up watching DiMaggio, Rizzuto, Berra, and Ford, who believed the Roger Maris single season homerun record of 61 would never be broken. This was before Sosa and McGwire.

My argument was clear. Players now train year-round; they lift repetitive weights so their bodies don't lose their "God given baseball skills," eat more protein, eat less pasta and other carbohydrates, take more vitamins, and keep their legs stronger than players of the past. There are fewer double-headers, easier and comfortable travel schedules, and easier day-night scheduling. Science and medical advances took quantum leaps in maintenance, prevention and injury recovery. All of these factors meant that it was only a matter of time before a player hit 70 homeruns. Furthermore, all of this weight training meant that players could hit more home runs to the opposite field, turning outs into homers, making 70 homers in a season more likely.

Steroids were not even a consideration in my debates with my father. Steroids was a football problem, marijuana was a basketball problem, but baseball seemed to just have a lot of guys who liked to drink a lot of beer, early 1980s cocaine scandal aside. I guess we really were quite naïve back in the 1990s stone age.

I thought McGwire and others to be perfectly legit. I wanted to believe just like every other fan that everything was on the up and up. I personally did not care if any player took any performance enhancement as long as it is USA Federal legal and I still feel that way today.

Illegal steroids are bad, dangerous, wrong and cheating. Players who cross the line destroy the fabric of the game and a representative of the deterioration of ethical behavior throughout our society. All other enhancements I am fine with, as an ongoing evolution of the athlete. Just as breaking the 4 minute mile was unthinkable but broken, I felt it would be natural for 70 homers to be broken.

Some General Managers essentially raised the white flag on illegal steroids for a combination of reasons; some level of naïve, the unknown macro impact and pervasiveness, the most powerful Union in the world resisted any pursuit of stifling policing policy, owners turning a blind eye because it was short-term revenue beneficial not to show the world its dirty laundry. Frankly, if they asked a player if they were taking steroids and they said no, then that was the end of the discussion. Even if the player's head bones were deforming and growing, and the player had characteristics of "'roid rage" the GM hands were tied.

So they let it go. They, in general, signed guys whether they suspected the use of steroids or not. Respectfully, I recognize that some GMs absolutely did not know. The public was not calling for anyone's head, no one was going to jail, the Unions pushed back on policing, the owners demanded success or they would change GMs.

I will not convict any player in this book who has not admitted or been convicted of using illegal steroids. I do point out that the current successful MLB team needs to be more street smart and less book smart on signing players on performance highs and then taking the hit and losing the player at their performance low. It's easier said than done but some may need more "get out of the swivel chair" foot work before raising the white flag.

Black and Blue Flag– Four Street Smart Signs MLB Trouble

There is a separate story, unfortunately pushed aside due to steroids that I find fascinating; a reflection on the evolution of nutrition, exercise, weight training, and training regimens. Legal advancements and lessons learned during the Steroid ERA also played a game changing role on players, teams, cities, and World Championships over the years as performance enhancements flipped decision making foundations from the mid 1980s to the 2008.

I've noticed three training and performance related impacts to the game not seen before the 1990s. This is not just about substance abuse. This is about overall training results and their impact on the playing field, how this impacted teams, and created new data mining disciplines that determine whether or not to sign players, for how much, and for what number of years. This is the GM Dilemma.

As I indicated at the beginning of this section, I don't profess to be right; I just want to get it right. We now know that players trained the "good' way, others through "bad" and "ugly" means. I never saw a player do anything illegal and I presume everyone on an individual, case by case basis, to be innocent unless admitted guilt or proven guilty. My observations are from a competitive perspective; the impact of all performance progress on management decision-making.

Unfortunately, as many stars have expressed their concern recently, it is unclear who to believe was innocent and who was guilty. As I've discussed in my other publications under other topics, if an employee provides me with 100 records, and indicates that 15 records are inaccurate but they are not sure which records they are, then I have no choice but to assume they are all inaccurate until proven otherwise. I will provide my observations and let you determine what to think.

Observation One -Re-curing One Year Crash and Burn

Mark McGwire – I was fascinated how Mark McGwire went from seasons of 58, 58, 70, 65 homerun seasons, followed by 32 homers with a .302 batting average, .483 OBP to…WHAM! .187 batting average and out of baseball! Holy Cow! That was shocking to me. He was only 38. What the heck happened in one off season?

Sammy Sosa – as Sammy grew over the years from what appeared to me in Texas to be a relatively skinny, strong player to this big, muscular giant with homerun totals of 36,40, 36, 66, 63, 50, 64, 49, 40, 35 (2004) to…WHAM! 14 homers, .221 batting average and .289 OBP. Out of baseball for 2005 season. Wow. The Baltimore GM had to have had many sleepless nights as he thought he was going to be able to compete with division rivals Yankees and Red Sox.

Chuck Knoblauch – All-Star, World Champion Yankee 2nd baseman suddenly comes up with stress related struggle with throwing the ball to first base, picks up in pressure-less Kansas City but still only hits .210 and is out of baseball after 2002 at 34 years old. What in the world happened? Was this mental or physical?

Jason Giambi – hits 43, 38, 41 with Oakland, signs monster contract with Yankees, hits 41 homeruns and then… (2004) WHAM! Misses most of season, says he caught a parasite in Japan back in March, hits 12 homeruns. People essentially believe his apology was essentially admitting to taking steroids but I don't want to interpret – just looking from a GM perspective.

I continue to look at all of these players and many more and I see a trend toward a performance cliff some players experience not seen in the pre-1990 athlete performance era. Not sure if it is triggered by the halting of the regimen or due to the extended continuance. My observation is that there is something impacting the body that leads some players to experience physical "crash and burn" that take them an entire year to recover.

I believe that there is a direct correlation between baseball players selecting some performance regimens not seen before 1990 that raises temporary performance to levels that follow a one year recovery period.

Observation Two– The Curious Case of Roger Clemens

Roger Clemens – I have made significant personal observations related to Roger Clemens, as a fan since the late 1990s. What stands out the clearest to me was how he got younger as his age went higher.

I remember watching Roger Clemens in 1996 and personally observing that he just might be near the end of his career. I thought he looked a little sluggish, losing velocity on his fast ball and might need to make adjustments that many pitchers need to make as they get older; move more to a finesse pitcher from a power pitcher.

If I understood the Red Sox correctly, they felt that they needed to let Clemens move on due to the balance of salary expectation, age and perceived performance probability. The Red Sox picked up Pedro Martinez at his prime the following year and let him go to the Mets when they felt they could not validate the salary he was able to garner from the Mets.

Roger Clemens went to the Toronto Blue Jays and two Hall-of-Fame 20 wins seasons. I admitted to myself at that point that I really had Roger Clemens wrong. I figured the Red Sox made another historic blunder letting him go but then tempered the loss with another pitching great in Pedro Martinez; not a bad trade off.

Then Clemens goes to the Yankees and lights up the American League and leads the team to two World Championships (much to the dismay of the Red Sox who still couldn't to that point win a darned World Series).

I honestly just felt that Roger Clemens, one of the greatest pitchers of all-time, was just a workaholic perfectionist just like Nolan Ryan. I was amazed at Nolan Ryan's work ethic. Roger Clemens was clearly dedicated to be a World Champion and to reach baseball immortal status. He had the competitive anger and was working harder than anyone else.

Roger then went to the Houston Astros and became even greater astonishment but I took it as "National League competition;" note to aging pitchers in the American League, go to the National League.

In the National League you have the pitcher in the 9th slot, usually a weak number 8 hitter, and relatively good but average 7 hitter. The American League is usually stacked from top to bottom. You get to the 9 hitter and he may be a 30-40 homer dude or .300 hitter. You can never let up. Your statistics are going to be a lot higher in the American League and you are always going to be in in-game trouble.

To me, Roger Clemens, 8 years after leaving Boston and after he was thought to be at the end of his career, was still at the top of his game because he worked so hard, because he was a baseball immortal and because he got to move over to the National League. It appeared the Red Sox (and I) misread the sell high point.

The current problems that Roger Clemens is dealing with related to performance enhancements are well documented and ongoing. I can't help but thinking way back when he was with the Red Sox and it seemed like he was nearing the end of his career, before Toronto, before New York, before Houston, and back to New York again for the $multi-million final season...

Observation Three– Good, Bad, Ugly; Texas Rangers

A significant amount of public attention has been directed at the 1990s-2000s Texas Rangers; Jose Canseco wrote the books calling out Palmeiro, Ivan Rodriguez and others, then Kevin Brown landed on the Mitchell report, and now Alex Rodriguez made his performance enhancement usage public acknowledgment.

I worked in the press box throughout the 1990s and I reflect on the players' training, weightlifting, nutrition, cycling, and even unique pitching exercises developed by Tom House. There were so many changes in performance development evolution for player off-field preparation not collectively seen in the 1970s and early 1980s.

I believe player conditioning reflected or directed the new age in public advancements about vitamins, carbohydrates, proteins, weightlifting, drugs and conditioning. I am a New York Italian and I remember cutting spaghetti dinners down from 5 nights a week to one. I began taking protein shakes before jogging. The country as a whole began to modify their diets and became increasingly educated on nutritional advancements.

I want to be clear. I am making observation of the Texas Rangers 1990s teams from a weightlifting and training perspective. I don't know who did what when, how often. I'll leave that to MLB, the courts and to Jose Canseco. Here is what fascinated me at that time from a training, nutrition, and on-field performance perspective. I believe this is important historical reflection because there was a clear evolution in player performance on the field. There were both good positives that are taken for granted now, as well as bad and ugly lessons learned along the way off the field still being sorted out today.

Before 1992 the only players I equated with weight lifting had been Ron Bloomberg, Greg Luzinski, and Carlton Fisk. What does stand out in my mind is that a number of the Rangers players returned from the off-season all, to me, "bulked up" from weightlifting.

2B Julio Franco was clearly more muscle bound from the previous season and he became a full-time Designated Hitter. The common belief in baseball was that if you lifted weights you would diminish your baseball skills. Here I am looking at, what I would term, a bulked up body-builder looking player who was moving from 2B to DH. Today weightlifting is common place in baseball. Also, respectfully Julio Franco, aside from missing the 1998 season and playing in one game in 1999, was still playing in 2007 at age 48 and may get a chance after 50! Amazing.

Dean Palmer – Dean had the most fascinating injury, to me, that I ever heard of in any sport, ever. He is at the top of my list for most curious injury. He swung the bat in a game against the Twins in 1995 and his bicep tore to what folks described at the time as "his muscle rolled up." I have never heard of that before or since. He swung the bat and let out a scream. I have seen so many injuries but never heard of anything like this. Dean was one of the good guys and it was shocking. Without that injury I wonder how much greater he would have been and what might have been during their playoff stretch.

Rafael Palmeiro – The only thing I'll say about Palmeiro is shock around the events that transpired with Canseco, the courts, and following events. He was never a big guy, or overly muscular. He never had the "roid rage" or anything that would put him on your radar. He was consistent, a great hitter, a clutch player. It was a shocking string of events in Baltimore at the end of a career for a proud and hard working person.

Ivan "Pudge" Rodriguez – Pudge has had a Hall-of-Fame career. He was also called out by Jose Canseco for using steroids. Pudge followed the great catcher, Jim Sundberg, in Texas.

The interesting observation on Pudge is that he was in contract negotiations with the Texas Rangers in 1997 and the Rangers were reportedly hesitant to pay him his marketplace value on a long-term contract. The reason that played out in the media was that the Rangers believed he was a great player but that his performance could potentially decline toward the end of an extended contract, at least in relation to the $millions they would need to pay for his performance.

The Rangers did their homework and determined that catchers tend to decline beyond the 1,000-game milestone. The catching position is the most brutal day-to-day position in baseball. The Rangers, as I understood the daily negotiations through the media, saw risk that Pudge could experience the natural breakdown that had occurred to so many great catchers in the history of the game. But Pudge was a hard worker who stayed in shape, stayed fit, stretched regularly, and arguably stayed physically healthier than any catcher in the history of the game. I remember reflecting on how far conditioning and health knowledge society and baseball had come since even the mid 1980s. I wanted the Rangers to sign Pudge. They did. Then he shows up in Jose Canseco's lineup of users.

Pudge later moved on to the Marlins for a season and Tigers for 4 ½ seasons and on to the Yankees. Throughout these years, every year, 12 years after that famous public negotiation between the Rangers and Rodriguez, I remark how amazing Pudge has arguably reached endurance and performance levels rarely seen before by the catcher position. He now surpassed the 2,000 game milestone. He is now in Carlton Fisk longevity standard measures; in the same class with one of the first weight training pioneers in Major League Baseball.

Juan Gonzalez – His career has been peculiar from statistical and injury perspectives. During his peak years Juan put up homerun seasons of 47, 42, 45, 39, 22 (115 games), 35, gets a $24million contract with the Rangers and…WHAM! He plays a grand total of 186 games and 37 homeruns total over the next 4 years for three teams and out of baseball. His last solid season was 32 years old. What the heck?! The Rangers ownership is on public record about its disappointment and concern about Juan's performance selections.

Jose Canseco and Kevin Brown were on those Texas Rangers teams and readers can read about them in the Joe Torre and Jose Canseco books, as well as the Mitchell report.

Observation Four– GM "Buy-Low, Sell-High" Dilemma

It is my hope that my first three observations are valuable insight into the burden, and high the stakes, on the General Manager shoulders to make the right signing decisions in the steroid through post-steroid era. The pressure on the players is equally great.

The performance enhancement issue plays a direct impact on the victory maximizing vs. the profit maximizing teams. The Yankees are not only the classic victory maximizing team, but also the poster child for buy high-sell low. Some of their mistakes are directly related to player performance driven roller-coasters because they often signed players coming off of their best seasons, in some cases artificially produced.

Included in the Mitchell Report are a number of Yankees on the list for Mitchell Report determined pre-Yankees years off the field activity which may or may not have changed the Yankees signing and/or salary offer decisions. I'm not sure how history may have played out in most cases but it may have changed the team mind about trading Soriano for A-Rod. They may have signed another player for Giambi and maybe that would have led to a World Championship or more. Would the team have signed Kevin Brown? We will never know.

On the flip side of the Yankees spending decisions, would the Boston Red Sox still be chasing their first World Series victory if the Yankees had signed non-Mitchell report related players for those $monster millions?

Players included in the Mitchell report include:

- Jason Giambi
- Gary Sheffield
- Roger Clemens
- Andy Pettitte
- Chuck Knoblauch
- Denny Neagle
- Mike Stanton
- Kevin Brown

Since then Alex Rodriguez made public acknowledgement after being called out as one of 104 players who failed a drug test, originally negotiated to stay forever untraceable and anonymous. At the time of this writing, there are 103 more names known not yet disclosed who did not pass 2003 drug tests. Is it possible that every top 10 performer of an entire decade represents that 103 player list? How many Texas Rangers? How many New York Yankees? How many Red Sox?

The Red Sox have been interestingly both successful and relatively steroid free, Donnelly, Vaughn and Gagne aside (assuming any potential Clemens issues are possibly post Red Sox related), during the steroid era. Are they loaded up on this list? Perhaps the Red Sox are plain and simply a lot smarter than the other GMs and they can see steroids use a mile away, they get out of their swivel chairs, see what is happening first hand, and can see what players not to go near. Until the names are released the innocent will be suspected with the guilty.

How many players only passed their tests because they knew enough and in well enough in advance, to pass their tests? What masking agents don't we know about? Who in MLB was in position to tip off players who turned up clean? How pervasive was this issue beyond 104 names in just one season? How many were guilty of using illegal substances vs. legal but banned substances?

Street smarts tells me to follow the money; where there are players making $25million yearly in a $multi-billion industry, there is a masking agent we don't know about and a Benedict Arnold tipping off a player of a coming test. When in doubt, follow the money.

At the end of the day, under normal competitive circumstances it is very difficult to make roster decisions regarding a player's current capabilities, studying past history, and projecting future capabilities. The revelation of how rampant player cheating was over the course of a 20 year period is alarming. I understand the frustration of the innocent when they hear "rampant." I get it. However, the impact has been significant to the tune of many $tens-millions. To the kids and working fans who don't come close to those salaries, and who wake up every day to read about how their favorite team and players did, this has been "rampant." When steroid users on another team kept their team out of the playoffs (and also cost the city $millions in revenue), it was rampant.

In addition to the player use, evidence seems to indicate that once a player moves to eliminate the use of some types of enhancement, the following pain to the player body, and residual impact to the city, fans, and management could last a year or more while the player returns to pre-enhancement form.

Whether on Wall Street or General Managing a Major League Baseball team, or even competing players, the game has been stacked against the people playing honestly to a different set of rules while others have made many $millions by cheating.

From a lessons learned perspective, the timeless lesson is that the General Manager must understand the true highs and lows, determine the risks, develop a risk mitigation plan in case the risks come to fruition, and execute as quickly as possible.

Art of the Long View

I utilize a technique that I learned back in the 1980s. It is based upon the book **"Art of the Long View" by Peter Schwartz**. If I remember correctly, this technique was first developed by Shell Oil in the 1970s.

Essentially, look to the future and determine the best case, worst case, and most likely scenarios moving forward. You proactively come up with an action plan for each scenario and readily act in the case that ultimately happens. I recommend all General Managers read "Art of the Long View." In this post steroid era (or just the dawn of the masking era?) the game is inevitably going to change again in unpredictable ways. The successful GMs will be those who can swiftly, proactively adjust to the changes; the ones who can swiftly change with the game, with an Art of the Long View will win.

Section 3 - Management Skills

Chapter 6:

The Versatile General Manager

Think about the various types of people you deal with at home, work and out in public every day. Now think about the daily interaction the MLB General Manager has with the different personalities in the team clubhouse. Each day throughout the year the General Manager has to deal with many groups including; the Union, all forms of home town and visiting media, ownership, fans, the team players, scouting department, often legal, finance and other departments, other GMs, player agents, and community groups.

In fact, every leader in every vertical industry needs to interact with people with differences, including beliefs, tendencies, and ways of managing stress. No leader can adequately navigate all business minefields without some level of understanding people. The importance of social styles dates back to Socrates and Plato.

About ten years ago I was fortunate to have been trained through CSC by Ridge Associates on their book, "People Style at Work." Some of their teaching is based on work developed by David W. Merrill, PhD. I am a student of this training, not a teacher so I will share with you what this training means to me and recommend that you expand the quality of your relationships by pursuing this further.

Essentially, from a 30,000 foot perspective, the discipline breaks social style into four core types, none of them any better than the other. Society needs every one of these styles for a healthy balance. People within each style have secondary tendencies regarding how they act and interact with others based upon internal beliefs and evolved characteristics.

Anaytic	Driver
Amiable	Expressive

People from each of these social styles essentially have primary, more extreme secondary tendencies related to how they want to be treated with respect, fairness and honesty.

Analytic **Analytic**	Driver		Analytic **Driver**	Driver
Amiable	Expressive		Amiable	Expressive

Analytic **Amiable**	Driver		Analytic **Expressive**	Driver
Amiable	Expressive		Amiable	Expressive

People also have different means of managing stress. Understanding this in depth provides individuals with the awareness of how others view these common needs, and the means that they themselves also want to be treated.

From the most basic perspective, as I understand social styles, everyone wants to be treated with a core set of values. How they view the meaning of these values and how to provide and receive these values in interacting with others; their view of the world, is the difference that most often creates conflict.

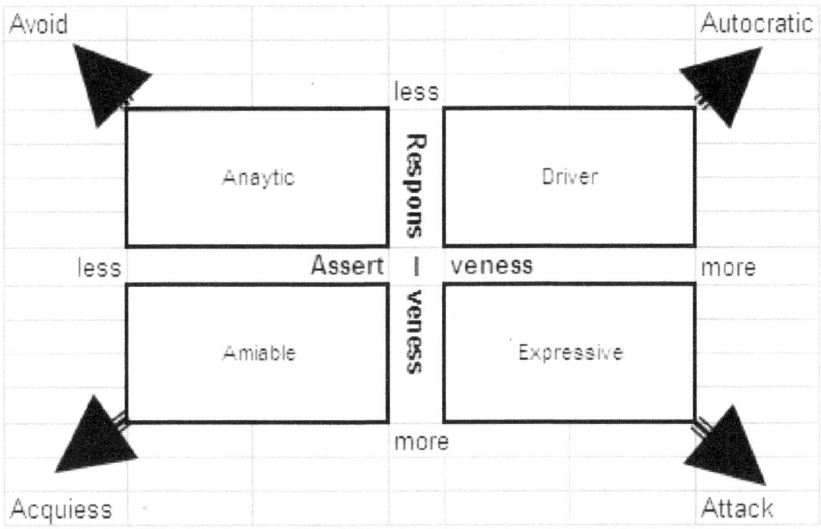

I have always been fascinated by an underlying "Z factor" that each social style follows in dealing immediate and life-long related conflict and stress.

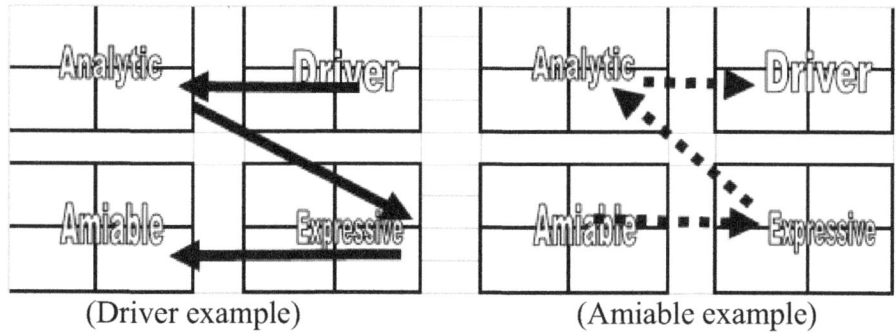

(Driver example)   (Amiable example)

Let's review a couple Z factor examples. The first is an example provided by Jim Bolton at Ridge Associates, to show how Richard Nixon did not stay in his typical Driver backup style during Watergate:

"As a Driver Nixon's first Backup was to become Autocratic—he mandated an executive sanction that he would not release the tapes. After public pressure he went to Avoidance—he retreated to Camp David for a couple weeks. As the public furor increased and the press hounded him, Nixon began to Attack—he fired the special prosecutor and damned the press (the Saturday Night Massacre). Many believe that he resigned in Backup— Acquiescing—responding to others' demands that he resign, yet not admitting any guilt."

I observe how Rafael Palmeiro went on the finger pointing attack, as an expressive, to congress denying ever taking steroids. Palmeiro then was quite amiable, volunteering to assist congressmen to cleanse baseball, and he then became determined in his denial as his past test results became known, until evidence was overwhelming. He then left baseball, out of the public eye and avoided all unwelcome publicity.

I believe Andy Pettitte is an Amiable. He was open from the beginning about substance use, avoided confrontation, then agreed to testimony to take control of the deteriorating situation; he put the truth, provided full disclosure about Roger Clemens. He removed himself from the public eye, even almost retired and he is now proactively authoritative.

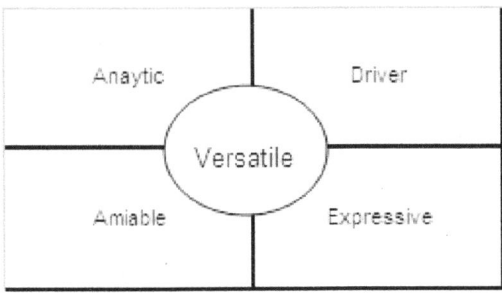

MLB General Managers, leaders in all vertical industries, and even all people in society have a great array of people they interact with throughout each day.

Understanding how people are socially and how they react to stress goes a long way to reducing conflict, understanding others, being more centrally versatile, garnering respect, to lead, and in creating a positive environment.

There is a significant amount more than what I only touch on here in this chapter but I hope I've shown how valuable this type of study can be on your career and social lives both at home and in the public. I recommend the "People Styles at Work" by Robert Bolton & Dorothy Grover Bolton. I also recommend corporate training from Ridge Associates.

BOOK II

Book II Introduction

Book II is the out of print first edition of my book, titled *The Official Book on the Business of Baseball General Management.*

The topics explored in this Book II are timeless and were written with the view that these were essential for the baseball General Manager, leaders in any field, and represented core economic labor concepts. For this reason, I provide this book as "Book II" in this Street Smart Sports Management book. Instead of having folks purchase two books I felt the value was to provide everyone with all expanded concepts under the framework of a single expanded book. I hope you find the value in this Book II as I did when developing the original book.

Scope – Who is Book II written for?

I made the decision that this book will present a management perspective to the business of baseball general management that uses financial, economic, and sabermetrics inputs to drive decisions based upon my philosophy of player resource management.

The scope for this book is all areas of **Business of Baseball General Management**. The book is sectioned into:

Section 4 - Working Management Model
This section is for any employee in any industry. It is a high level, "20,000 foot" view of core management discipline and methodology foundation. Regardless of the industry, company, or corporate culture, the successful manager can build a core foundation that will instill confidence and stability.

Readers can become better managers by implementing the principles that I cover in this section and focus through deeper training and reading in the areas I cover in this section.

If you want to a become Baseball General Manager or become a better one, this section will give you an essential base toolkit of skills. The high pressure, high stakes position is a combination ambassador, politician, corporate leader, psychologist and lawyer. A core set of these disciplines and values outlined here is the foundation for success.

Section 5 - Strategy for Building a Winning Baseball Team

THIS IS THE AREA in the book which most people think of when wanting to know about the pure "baseball" areas of baseball management. Field management, scouting, player and team assessments are covered in this section. Most baseball fan readers want to know this information because it is what most fans are familiar with when watching games at the ballpark, on TV, reading magazines and newspapers, and talking baseball with other fans at the sports bar, the office and coffee shops.

For the person who wants to become a General Manager (GM), this section details the baseball focus in which the successful GM must be skilled and disciplined.

I do not drive into deep sabermetrics research. Sabermetrics is a contributing input into the management resource decision making but not the sole basis for my analysis. I have read and studied many baseball books available that relate to sabermetrics. Rather than focus on these inputs in my book, I included my library of baseball sabermetrics, history and strategy books, which I recommend for additional research, in the Baseball Library section at the back of this book.

Section 6 - Major League Economics Factors
This section is written for readers who want to obtain their degree in sports management. At the doctorate level, economics and statistics are core courses.

This is also for the individuals who want to understand the advanced economic constraints in the eternal debate over labor value and rewards. After reading this section the reader will have an expanded view, beyond the passions, opinions, and politics focus in current public debates; I present a unique slant on what the core factors are to baseball labor valuation, and insight into contracts decision making.

Objective

Today sabermetrics is the buzz word throughout baseball. There are many fascinating books, and significant focus on the internet, print and television media, board games and established rotisserie leagues, all related to baseball sabermetrics. Long a rotisserie fan tool, the explosion of sabermetrics popularity in the Major Leagues was brought on by the best selling book Moneyball, which presented the A's as the anti-rich team success story through sabermetrics. The successful rise of the Red Sox, led by sabermetricians Bill James, Theo Epstein and others, pushed sabermetrics even further into the forefront of baseball management theory.

I gained my first insight and respect for statistical baseball measures back in the summer of 1973 when I played an entire 1971 Sports Illustrated Baseball season for all 24 teams. I kept offense and pitching statistics for every player on every team on paper, using pencils, erasers, and scratch paper to calculate player and team totals. Calculators and computers were not options back then.

During the season, I used pitching rotations, and made strategic decisions based upon specific player skill sets, pitcher-batter righty-lefty match ups, and base-stealing percentages vs. defensive strength. The only player I would intentionally walk throughout the league was Willie Stargell because he hit over 70 homeruns for the Sports Illustrated World Series winning Pirates.

The most significant impact sabermetrics has made on the game today, I believe, is that proven statistical minds from Wall Street, Stats Inc., Baseball Prospectus and others have successfully replaced the use of basic statistics by some teams for competitive advantage over past decades and eras with the creation of advanced linear information to give some baseball teams a new short-term competitive advantage.

These people kicked the door open for instant access to incredible variations of baseball data, creating linear insights to improve odds for short-term strategic success and potentially long-run success at player drafts and development. The ante has been raised; the bar is higher for management to make wiser field competition and player decisions.

However, all teams today utilize sabermetrics in various ways and each team now has one proprietary statistical tool or another. Teams have had time to observe and adjust to which sabermetrics proved to be successful. Some teams will continue to have brighter minds and strategies for using the data but sabermetrics by itself, essentially rotisserie, will not bring success. Some baseball people are currently de-emphasizing the Moneyball version of sabermetrics. The Braves are considered to be the anti-Moneyball team.

The new competitive advantage, I believe, is the emphasis of a general management and scouting working model based upon a unified business discipline and baseball philosophy supported by sabermetrics.

For this reason, this book's objective is to define, implement and enforce a working model for the business of baseball management discipline and classic baseball philosophy that is supported by economics, finance, and baseball sabermetrics instead of the currently popular replacement of the discipline and philosophy with rotisserie-like use of sabermetrics.

Section 4 - Management Working Model

Working Management Model (for managers in any industry)

1. Disciplined Management of Triple Constraints

In order to establish a winning MLB team I believe the organization needs to adhere to a disciplined prioritization and management of triple business constraints:

Budget

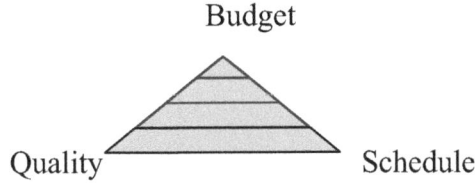

Quality   Schedule

- Budget: How much is the team willing to spend (top priority of profit maximizing teams and small market clubs)?

- Quality: What level of proven talent does the team want on the field?

- Schedule: How long is the team willing to take to develop a winning team (emphasized by victory maximizing teams like the Yankees)?

There is no way to avoid the triple constraints:
- If the team decreases its budget, it will impact the level of effort to replace top tier players.

- If the team moves from a 3 year goal to build a team through the farm system into a win-it-all team this year, then the team will need to place greater effort on quality and increase cost.

- If the team increases importance on top tier talent or to keep current stars from entering the free market, then the team will need to increase cost.

The triple constraints, directly or indirectly defined by the team owner, set the foundation for the organization decision making structure. The constraints provide direction for fiscal discipline, organizational philosophy, and guidelines for player transaction and development.

In a perfect world I would inherit a team that wants to win today, has a rich farm system, a talent rich MLB roster that matches up perfectly with our competition and plays with impeccable fundamentals and baseball intelligence, an unlimited budget, top notch Manager and coaching staff, great scouts and minor league teachers and lots of luck.

Since this is not a perfect world I would, as a General Manager, need to build organization chemistry and vision through defined discipline and philosophy. I would reinforce the vision through communication, core values and by surrounding myself with career baseball people loyal to the organization's vision.

2. Disciplined Organization Culture

Major League Baseball is a volatile environment. Competition is fierce. The stakes are great. In baseball, inherently a game of streaks, measurement of success is a moving target on a daily basis for fans, media and organization employees.

The respected General Manager needs to represent a stable organization culture through:

- **Conflict Discipline**
  - In order to stay the long-term course and maintain triple constraint discipline, the General Manager needs to have a versatile social style when dealing with the owner, players, agents, other General Managers, scouts, development personnel, fans, the media, and other organization departments.

    The training that I received breaks down social styles into expressive, driver, analytic, and amiable. I recommend that the reader do a web search or ask the local school or company training department about this type of training. What I find extremely useful and fascinating is that, if you can define a person's social style, through training you can understand what stress level the person is functioning in, and then you can better manage conflict to positive resolution.

  - Lead by example especially during stressful periods. Be solution oriented during rough stretches.

  - Open door policy – being available at all times.

- **Core Values**

There are countless variations of core values defined in companies and developed throughout an individual's growth. As long as the core values are adhered to when the going gets tough, not just lip service when times are good, I support this value discipline. The core values that were instilled in me, which I still speak to in and out of work, especially when stressful situations challenge and stretch individual's patience and reasoning:

- Partnership
- Innovation
- Excellence
- Respect

As long as an individual identifies core values and understands each core value in substance, then they can use whatever brings positive energy and results into their world.

- **Earning clear owner support.**

- The successful General Manager needs a top-down organization that is willing to implement and embrace the defined discipline and philosophy in order to succeed. Clear support from the owner is essential.

Direct open ownership support is the General Manager's most valuable conflict tool.

- Successful working models take time and there are often road bumps on the way. Players go into slumps, teams go through bad stretches, injuries can mount, luck can turn bad, and so many other possibilities.

When things don't go as perfectly as designed, ownership needs to have confidence and patience in the management team. The owner can only be expected to maintain the triple constraint course and stick with the current General Manager if provided with the basis for key decisions.

- Owners want to know about risk and return on investment. Present the facts to the owner. Owners want to minimize risk but risk is a necessary evil to achieve greater return on investment.

  The General Manager needs to win ownership confidence that the risk is educated and, baseball's driving intangible factor of chance (injury, ball bad bounce, umpire call, family tragedy, first bad year by the player, etc.) aside, the collection of decisions will bring a consistent winner.

- **Strong communication skills:**
  - Debrief the owner, and work with the scouting leadership and the development personnel in terms of the triple constraints discipline and working model. As a business leader, I expect two things regarding information from my team:

    1. It's not just the information communicated. It's the confidence level in the information communicated. Be able to speak to how you got the information, and be able to show a clear audit trail if the source turns out to be inaccurate. Otherwise, tell me it's a work in progress. Lack of confidence or knowledge of where the information was gathered is useless to me.

       If I'm told that 1 "fact" in a list of 10 is inaccurate but it is unclear which 1 of the 10 is inaccurate, then I consider all 10 to be false until proven otherwise.

2. I don't like surprises. Set expectations and calibrate expectations as often as necessary. I don't need a blow by blow debrief of progress but I need to know ASAP when developments impacting tactical, operational or strategic initiatives change. Timeliness is as important as the information. For example, if I find out after a trading deadline that a certain player from a region in the country is struggling to adapt to living in another region, and that my team knew but didn't tell me, what good is the information now? I cannot emphasize this strongly enough; don't catch your boss by surprise at the last minute, setting their expectation that all is well.

Scenario 1: Project A has problems and the team keeps leadership informed of the risks, assumptions and known issues, with a game plan for each, and one of the items still goes wrong. Leadership will likely have confidence in the team and appreciate the feedback. The leadership will take into account they were kept informed of the issue.

Scenario 2: Project B has the same problems, risks, assumptions and known issues as Project A. However, B doesn't inform leadership until it's too late. I am telling you there will be hell to pay.

Recap: Two identical situations, two separate outcomes driven by communication or lack thereof.

- Communicate with the core baseball experts in the organization in terms of the working model for player selection, development and transactions. What this means is that everyone in the organization has a clear baseline of scope boundaries under which you work. Decision criteria, methodology and discipline, as well as clear vision and mission should be clearly understood by your loyal team. All discussions and debate relate to those boundaries.

- Communicate with the media and fans regularly on why the team is making certain transactions and why others are avoided. I believe fans and media will at least respect decisions if they believe you are committed to winning and you confidently present a game plan for success based upon defined constraints (i.e. market revenue management limits balanced by developing talent and level of risk and downsides to avoiding publicly perceived transaction opportunities).

- One significant caveat: the other General Managers are listening closely to everything you publish, speak, and refer to. There are many disclosures, sources of information, strategies, and endless scenarios of tactical and operational moves that you cannot reveal to your competition. Much of the information to the media and fans will either have to be carefully presented or explained after the fact. The best way to manage this is to provide a limited view of your core vision.

- **Set achievable expectations.**
Promising 120 victories or increasing revenue by 300% is setting the team up to fail.

- **Share recognition.**
This includes staff, scouts, players, anyone. Ronald Reagan enjoyed giving all of the credit to his team. Employees rate appreciation and recognition as top priorities.

- **Include experts on decisions** (but maintain clearly that the final decision is yours).
  - The General Manager should include the career baseball subject matter experts (SMEs) on all transaction decisions, while maintaining the basis of core constraints. Making educated decisions from a culture of due diligence rather than by going it alone builds loyalty and respect, and builds support when answering to the media, fans and owner on decisions.

    However, you have got to be careful to maintain authority. The team must know that once the debate is over, that you will make the ultimate decision, and the team must embrace the decision as though it was their own.

  - Continuity brings great players into the minor league system which builds development. Reward loyalty. Embrace legacy. Maintain a close culture.

- **Competence:**
  - More damaging to credibility than presenting incorrect facts is to be in the dark of how the facts you present were collected.

  - When asked a question, "I don't know" is more important than making an uncertain response.

  - Strong negotiation skills. Know the numbers.

  - Continually listen and learn from the experts.

  - Maintain daily attention to detail. The General Manager needs to build a disciplined, knowledgeable management team that is on top of all competing team player moves and issues, as well as league player availability – getting guys off of wire services, protecting own players, etc. One team lost a future All-Star to another team when they dropped the ball and lost him in the Rule 5 draft. This should never happen. It is the management equivalent to a game day mental error that will haunt the team every game for years.

  - Associative knowledge is not a replacement for quantifiable understanding of factors that impact the General Manager's decisions.

3.   Philosophy of Effective Management

Organization disciplined culture and constraints are more easily sustained with a strong management philosophy. I believe that you make your own luck. All battles are won and lost, not in the competition, but in the preparation. Before a team starts a season or game, that team has already won or lost in the preparation. Preparation includes both quantifiable attention to detail and the intangible building of strong leadership character.

You don't make decisions from a swivel chair.

All employees taking ownership, taking action to determine ways to win is paramount to me. I always keep in mind a famous story about US General Patton in World War II.

Essentially, as legend has it, General Patton asked his strategists which part of a river the troops and tanks should cross before positioning for a battle. Being loyal, hard working soldiers, they immediately went to work on their maps to determine their proposed solution.

A few hours later General Patton, wet up to his thighs, walked in and indicated that they would cross the river at a deep river point because the ground was rocky and solid. He indicated that the more desirable shallow area was too muddy and tanks could get stuck. When asked how he was so sure, he indicated that he walked across the river at both points. Patton is to have said that *you don't make decisions from a swivel chair.*

Counting on answers about players who will determine your job security, the victory and revenue success of an organization, and the image of a city through just charts and scores, phone calls, and second hand opinions to me is not ethical.

The enemy has an Army too.
I believe in strength, composure, and leadership by example when execution goes less than 100% as planned.

In baseball, management job security is fragile. The General Management, the Scouting and Player Development departments are continually at odds by design.

The Scouts find all of the reasons why a player should be drafted, and ultimately are responsible for most draft day decisions. Player Development, tasked with grooming these players from minor leaguers to winning major leaguers, finds all of the reasons why these players lack the qualifications to make it to "The Show."

Meanwhile, the General Management makes the judgment call on player transactions. All groups are under pressure, and when a player is cut or traded, is it because the General Manager moved too quickly, or because he never should have been drafted, or because Development did not progress the player to his potential?

Because the player draft-to-majors success rate is less than 10%, and because so many teams go from spring time contenders to perceived disappointments, I believe the management team needs to be a strong, composed and supportive team especially when there is disagreement.

The pressures on the team and low success ratios are experienced throughout the league every season to the rich, the poor, the weak and the strong teams. Teams with strong leadership who can breed confidence through the ranks, the organization, the fans and the media are the teams that can make the difficult decisions that ultimately sustain winning teams.

This brings to mind a World War I story regarding General Pershing. Essentially, before a battle, Pershing is said to have sent an analyst out to assess troop preparedness. At the end of the day the analyst came back visibly shaken. He indicated a list of concerns such as: Many bullets did not match the rifles, shortages in tank replacement parts, discrepancies in food rations, and other issues on a long list of concerns. Pershing reviewed the list, expressed his appreciation for the hard work and is said to have expressed another variation of his famous "don't worry" lines; pointedly telling the analyst not to worry...*not to worry because the enemy had an army too.* In baseball, everybody else has a team too.

The Baseball Turtle with the Ticker

A General Manager needs to recognize which players will lead during the competition when the summation of business of baseball moves is in the hands of men on the playing field.

I need to reference high school in order to tap into the most extreme deviation in perception vs. result in player talent that I have ever seen. The player, a Toms River HS South baseball player named Marty Donato, made the single greatest impact on my judgment of talent to this day. Marty was short, ran turtle-like 40 and 60 yard dashes, and fully qualified for his nickname, The Turtle.

During practices we would have to run laps around the field. Marty was so slow that our fastest players would lap him regularly. No one really noticed or cared too much since Marty was a catcher, a stereotypically slow position. We also knew he was not slacking because he was too competitive to not run full speed at all times.

What Marty lacked in speed he made up for in high IQ and baseball IQ (baseball intelligence). Even greater than his instincts and studies of baseball techniques and strategy was his competitive anger that we called The Ticker (heart driven to succeed). Marty was clearly a leader hell-bent on winning.

Marty's ticker drove him to replace his "turtle" speed with base running intelligence. Probably one of the slowest starting players the school produced over the past twenty years, he stole all 12 bases he attempted that season.

Twelve for 12 on the base paths in the league that produced such Major League players as Jeff Musselman, Mark and Al Leiter, and loaded with players from teams like the Little League World Series Champions Lakewood and Toms River.

The key lesson I learned was that baseball intelligence separates the winners and losers. Baseball intelligence equals speed. Speed creates runs. Lowering the risk to manufacture runs through speed creates victories.

On paper Marty should not have been a starting player. Baseball intelligence and a ticker which does not show up on paper, I believe, are the differentiators during the demanding 162 game season the post-season. The General Manager should stay out of the swivel chair in order to find that type of player.

Section 5 - Baseball Strategy

Strategy to Building and Maintaining a Winning Major League Baseball Team

Tom Landry, the Hall of Fame Coach of the Dallas Cowboys once indicated that he had been considered a genius during 20 years of playoffs and success but a couple down years and suddenly he was identified by some in the media as unqualified to coach. The only difference was whether or not he had the talent to execute his plays.

As the General Manager I would want to have my players, Managers and coaches in place that make me look like a genius.

My model for on field success is based upon:
- ☑ Laws of supply and demand, fiscal responsibility, and free market principles.
- ☑ Winning through personnel with loyalty, shared vision, strong fundamentals, sense of ownership, intelligence, and competitive anger.
- ☑ A list of team considerations, which will be revealed in this section, that provides winning intangibles to building a team.

Everything provided in this section leads to my high level baseball strategy overview; achievement starts and ends with one principle:

Every success is gained or lost in the preparation. You make your own luck. Every victory is won or lost before the game even starts; it's all in the preparation.

1. Field Management philosophy

- All ships in one direction. Hire a loyal Manager and coaches who embrace our game strategy philosophy and utilize role players the way we envision when making transactions (including draft picks):
  - **Run maximization.**
  A Manager, who only bunts with the weak hitter, does not give outs away, goes with the run and hit but not much hit and run. Essentially, the Manager view of strategy is similar to the Earl Weaver baseball strategy.

  - **Win maximization.**
  A Manager who will not rest half his team in the second game of a double header. This drives me insane! I cannot believe that players cannot compete twice in one day every now and then. Teams play for weeks at a time to make up ground or get a game breathing room. To lower the odds of winning a second game of a doubleheader is incomprehensible to me!

  - **Player maximization.**
  A Manager needs to have my philosophy of how to use the players we provide. I refer to Earl Weaver as a master of utilizing player strengths. Use a four-man starting pitching staff vs. the popular five-man rotation, manage the game to place role players in strategically advantageous match ups, run and hit (vs. hit and run), uses sabermetrics related to our team vs. the opposition, while ignoring statistics based upon how opposing players fared against other teams other than our own. I believe, due to all of the intangible luck and situational factors, statistics in non-current team match-ups are irrelevant in game-day strategy.

- **Coaching as a competitive advantage.**
  When the Yankees moved Rodriguez to 3rd base they brought in Craig Nettles to teach him how to play. Tino Martinez and Jason Giambi were struggling at the plate so they brought in Don Mattingly. There should be an entire book written specifically on the value of coaches in the organization. The Yankees should be the model.

On the flip side, the Mets moved Mike Piazza to first base; the general perception was that the Mets and Keith Hernandez could not get him trained properly. Regardless of the reasons, ultimately I believe the training was less than successful.

There are always two sides to a story but bottom line is that good coaching is the only story for successful teams. Braves pitching, Red Sox hitting, Dodger Rookie-of-the-Year winners all lead back to good coaching.

My observation: I would always see Reggie Jackson, Yogi Berra and others in the clubhouse. Their knowledge is priceless. I believe that Jorge Posada could make the Hall of Fame in part due to the baseball elder wisdom around the clubhouse daily.

- **Defense maximization.**
  - I include intentional walks in the defense category. I equate intentional walks to a football team giving up first downs on penalties and turnovers. A base is a precious commodity. To give up 25% of your bases by intentional walk is self-defeating penalty. On top of that, analysis shows that pitchers often walk the guy after the intentional walk!

    No one can convince me that intentional walks, as common practice, is defense wise. Players with less than 40% success rate of getting on base are given a 100% free pass to first base. Las Vegas grows rich at 51% and above.

- I equate errors to a football team turning the ball over:

Errors are going to happen. They are a part of the game because physically humans are not machines.

Fielding errors can be decreased by the talent the Manager is able put on the field. A great fielding team reduces pitch counts, makes pitchers look stronger, reduces residual seasonal stress on the relief staff, takes pressure off the offense to score additional runs every day, and adds wins.

Mental errors are unacceptable. Mental errors occur when the player is not focused on his responsibility during these few hours in a day. Mental errors, like eyes are to the soul, reveal greater issues with the player and the team.

2.   Transaction philosophy

- Don't be the Yankees farm team. If you have four Yankees rejects in your starting lineup, there is a good chance you can't beat the Yankees head-to-head.

- Buy low, sell high for average players without exceptional or high demand tools. The laws of supply and demand pertain to players, and equity market principles pertain to player salaries.

- Value the potential return on free-agent investment vs. the risk of losing draft picks. In general, avoid signing free agents unless they are critical components to the team makeup.

- Don't lose a player without getting equal or better. Buy low, sell high:

  When considering not re-signing a star player, is the compensatory draft pick better than the player value?

  When considering not re-signing an average player, is the player easily replaceable?

  Make a trade before teams determine that you are willing to lose the player to the market place. This could mean trading the player a year sooner than you would prefer in order to maximize return.

  Do all that is possible to sign key players before the final year of the contract. Player contracts historically continue to go up. Over paying one year can look like a bargain the next, so just pay it now.

- Do not trade or sign free agents players with track records for being difficult, or those who have agents who are militantly insensitive to realistic player market value, and/or spirit of negotiation partnership.

- Stock up on in-demand player skills to add incentive and value to make future impact trades. For example, when maintaining part-time role players and AAA players, go after left handed pitchers who have been less than successful in other organizations. I go back to my strong belief in laws of supply and demand to strengthen a team through buy low, sell high principles.

- Forget pocket cost. Cut your losses instead of chasing past money. Whether on Wall Street or in a Casino, veterans know not to chase losses based on pocket cost. In baseball, if a costly player clearly does not work out, get best value possible immediately, move on.

- Adjust to teams in the division and league who clearly have players locked up for competitive advantage. Solid teams that don't match up well with key competitors are set up to fail. An example, NL East teams needed to assume over the past 16 years that the Braves have pitching and smart management.

- Know which teams are vulnerable. Look for good players in bad places. Buy low, sell high.

- Value in numbers plural, not number singular:
  - If a player wants a salary that has significant impact on the overall percentage of team salary, then it is time to move that player. It is not about whether or not the player is worth the money. It is about what the team can afford, what performance and injury risk it is willing to accept, and value the team expects from the player vs. the risk and expected value the team will get for multiple players instead of the one player.

  - If the owner is not going to increase the budget and pay the free market supply/demand rate for that scarce commodity, pitching, the GM needs to avoid higher priced players in order to increase the quality of the team's bottom talent 10%.

  For example, if a team has a circa $90million payroll, $3.3million average salary, $2.5million median salary. The only player making over $10million needs to be a solid producer or the team will be at a disadvantage.

  Meanwhile, the bottom 10% (three players at any given day on the seasonal 25 man roster) needs to out produce the other teams to offset the talent disadvantage at the top.

- I never understand when teams decide to trade away their best players in an effort to *improve*. The team that stands out in my mind, but by no means is alone, is the Texas Rangers. The Rangers lost a couple years to the Yankees in the playoffs. The team played solid but couldn't score against the eventual World Champion pitching staff.

Ownership decided to start over and got caught in the trap of diminishing their strength, trading away their best players. Keep the strength and improve the bottom 10%! If you lost a couple of times in the playoffs, *add* to the budget for the missing guy or two!

3. Pitching, pitching, and more pitching philosophy

- Pay for elite relief pitchers. Nothing is worse than spending all day building a lead or playing a tight game, while also waiting for the inevitable shelling of your relief staff.

- Minimize risk of injuries. Pitching injuries are inevitable. Sabermetrics, scout reviews of mechanics, grading of player size, strength, exercise, eating habits, stretching, etc. must all be used in assessing and keeping pitching talent. Pitching dominates the game; extra money goes to pitching, so attention to pitching preparation and commitment to detail need to be the highest priorities.

- Grab left handed pitchers when other teams are vulnerable. Everybody always needs another lefty pitcher. Stock pile every way possible. Other teams can always be enticed into a trade with that extra lefty carrot. When in doubt, add a lefty to your team or into the minor leagues.

- Select pitchers who throw many innings. Wear and tear on the staff due to one or more pitchers lacking in quality innings likely will cost the team games in August, September and October.

- Select pitchers who pitch. Pitchers should get high percentage ground balls and strikeouts, low on walks. Mistakes need to be singles, not homers. This philosophy starts with the yearly draft.

- Pitching model unlike the Texas Rangers. Offense is exciting but it never wins. One 1985 summer day sitting in the bleachers at Arlington Stadium, I heard casual fans say that the Texas Rangers would never win a championship because they don't believe in pitching, they just want to out hit opponents. Why fans get it but management doesn't is a mystery.

- Whatever the team budget is, convince management to spend $10million more on previously proven veteran pitchers. The money will usually come back in the stands through the win column. Convince ownership that the fixed budget must be padded by a variable $10million for additional pitching to increase revenue (wins = higher TV ratings, more fans at the stadium, more revenue).

The owner is concerned with profit. The owner sets a budget that equates to the expected revenue. If the owner can be convinced that the move will increase revenue, then he will meet his profit expectations. If you go to the well once and fail, then the expanded budget request will likely not be approved the next time.

## 4.	Player-type philosophy

- Hitters, who know the strike zone, can spray the field, with few strikeouts (except homerun hitters).

- Steal percentage leaders.

- Whether they steal 5 bases or 100 bases, it is competitively key in a game separating players and teams in terms of percentages that the base runner is nearly always safe.

- Leaders.
Some players lead by example, others by talent, others by attitude, by sacrifice and preparation. Everyone on the team must find their own way of leading. Leaders find reasons to win every day. I believe there was a certain leadership "magic" to the 1969, 1973, 1986 New York Mets. Somehow that magic pendulum that was unique and "You Gotta Believe!" patented by the Mets for the first 44 years swung to the extreme dark side in 2007. Regardless of the outcome, Mets ownership was wise to keep Willie Randolph in that role because he is a winner and the players on that roster need that same captain to reverse the unfathomable 2007.

- Players who step out of the dugout like they own the visitor field; players who act like they own the place. The psychological advantage leads to confidence, which leads to victories.

- Tickers (Heart!). Attitude. Players with heart and competitive anger even when scores are lopsided.

- Players who make opposition pitching mistakes become runs. Baseball is a game determined by pitchers. The greater the talent, including the playoffs and World Series, the fewer mistakes opponent pitchers will make. I believe that is why so many statistically solid offenses fail in post season. I want players who make pitchers pay. I don't care if they hit .390 against average to lower tier teams. I need the guy who takes pitches, fouls off tough pitches, and puts the one mistake into the peanut gallery.

- Sabermetrics friendly for our team.
  Use statistics to select players who fare well in specific roles on our team, and against teams and players that we will play against, at different ballparks. For example, if we are going to play against the Braves 19 times, I want to know how our players match up specifically against the Braves. If a player has a life-time on-base-percentage of .450 but is .190 against the pitchers in our division, then he is likely setup to fail so we should attempt to trade (sell) while his value is high.

- Diamond in the rough.
  Ask our scouts and coaches why some players on other teams are NOT doing well. Is it a batting stance, the city they are in, the opposing coaching staff, women problems, etc? The player who stands out greatest in my mind is the Red Sox David Ortiz. Although feedback in the press rooms was that the Twins couldn't give him away, the Red Sox saw something in his swing. Now he is a potential Hall of Famer.

- Can they play in the city?
  Some players excel because there is no pressure to win. Other players need a winning environment to excel. Can they handle irrational media and fans? Will they be happy in a rural city with limited off-field options or inter-personal feedback? Many cultural factors need to be considered.

- Avoid potentially negative clubhouse players. No exceptions. Some teams can handle a gifted star who seems to bring controversy. Most teams cannot. The Phillies cannot afford to get into a situation like the one the Eagles and Owens got into. The long grueling season, 162 game schedules are too difficult.

- Role players. I really don't care about the five tool guy. He's going to wind up playing on the Yankees for $20 million anyway. Give me the guy who does one or two things great, is baseball smart, comes to play.

- Keep the players you have but don't buy high, sell low. Especially at midseason when teams panic or give in to greater long term risk.

- Tie breakers.
  Playoffs and World Series are luck driven but pitching and defense increase your chances. Great pitching and defensive plays bring down offensive clubs. If two excellent hitters are available, and one plays better defense, then pay more the better defensive player.

- Legitimate signing potential.
  Who is their agent? What is their market value? Do they want to play here? What is their length of MLB service? What is their bargaining position-talent gap, etc?

5. Players draft philosophy

- College players. To me, high school players are too high of a risk and expect too high a price.

- Baseball players vs. athletes. I would count on and respect feedback from the scouting department. What I would focus on is the exceptional feedback about a player with one exceptional baseball skill. I would look for the player with fluid motion, natural movement, and natural, non-conscious mechanical effort. Foot speed, bat speed, mental adjustment to the strike zone and opposing pitch selections. One extreme example I would look out for is a hitter who can consistently hit the opposite field corner (fair territory). I want guys who have specific ways to beat you.

- Watch (and listen at) batting practice. Look for ease of movement, leadership, focus, wrist and foot speed, eyesight, who wears contact lenses, who stays out at night, who has a volatile personal life, who can steal signs? What are other players saying about him while he hits?

- Martino's Baseball IQ test. Players are currently given a battery of physical and mental tests. I would implement a time-intensive written and video test that measures their knowledge of game in-play situations. I would give high priority to their understanding of baseball in action strategy.

- Major League talent vs. Minor League talent.
There is a place for baseball franchise players. I would prefer franchise players over players with less potential. From a talent perspective, I want to know if a guy can hit the ball a mile (minor league talent) or turns pitching mistakes into homeruns (major league talent).

- Mechanics.
The New York Mets, already bitten by past injuries to potential pitching stars as Bill Pulsipher, Jason Isringhausen, and others, are said to have determined there was enough risk in Scott Kazmir pitching mechanics to play a role in trading him away. Interestingly, the Mets invested in Pedro Martinez, who has Hall of Fame mechanics, missed a significant number of games. There is no equation for if or when a pitcher could get injured or lose effectiveness. Teams need to improve their luck by enforcing strict mechanics guidelines.

Some baseball people were said to have predicted the injuries to Kerry Wood and other Cub pitchers because of their mechanics. I want to avoid signing what I believe to be high mechanics-driven risk players.

6.   Most valuable talent today (supply and demand)

- Catcher who calls and plays a baseball intelligent game.

- Next is the reliable "Mariano Rivera" type relief pitcher. Baseball is a league separating teams by percentage points. Just a single 9th inning loss per month puts a team six games in the hole. Losing games in the 9th is hell on earth.

- Next is the top-tier left handed pitcher.

- Next is a solid base stealer.
A guy who makes defenses move opens holes for hitters and starts rallies. However, outs are a precious commodity and the lowest risk runners (rarely caught stealing) to me are the only valuable base stealers.

- Next are players who can hit the opposite way. I love situational hitters.

- Next are strong pinch hitters and role players.
There are many pinch hitters and role players of relatively equal quality in the game. Rosters fill up with average supporting cast. I want the role players who are best at one thing. Even if the one thing is bunting, maybe warning track fly balls (game winning sacrifice fly guarantee), walks, run and hit, five innings of relief every two days, etc. Maybe it is stealing signs. Especially if it is stealing signs! I played against Admiral Farragut. They had a player whose only role was to sit at the end of the bench and decipher the opposition signs.

7.   The personality of my desired team lineup

- Power hitter in the outfield, third base or first base.
I believe that a team that counts on a power hitting shortstop or catcher is set up to fail in September due to wear and tear at their positions (taking them out of 2nd games of doubleheaders does not make them feel better!). Additionally, national league teams don't have the benefit of the designated hitter to rest catchers. Taking power out of the lineup for 10-20 games a year is costly in a league decided by percentage points.

- Other than the power hitter, the lineup should be stocked:
  - Walk a lot or make pitchers throw a lot of pitches without the hitter striking out. Pitchers determine games. Hitters need to capitalize when pitchers make mistakes. The more pitches a pitcher throws, the increased odds that he will make a mistake. The more pitches a pitcher throws, and more pitchers an opposition in your division needs to throw on any given day, the more it impacts their pitching staff over the coming games. I call it the "trickle down" theory of pitching economics through hitting discipline. Additionally, defenses get distracted and less sharp when they are watching a lot of pitches to each batter.

    My favorite un-appreciated player of all time <u>was Mickey Tettleton.</u> I loved watching him when he played for the Texas Rangers. He had a low batting average but he gave the pitchers fits and walked often. I covered the Rangers 81 home games a season and I can tell you confidently that his presence was a greater impact than other high profile guys on that team.

- Low percentage double play guys. Outs are the most precious commodity.

- Low strikeout guys aside from the power hitter or guys who don't work pitch counts unless they have high on-base percentages (on base percentage overrides at-bat pitch counts). These are guys who make pitchers make mistakes.

- Solid defense. For infielders this means range, double play capability (technique and arm strength) and error percentage. For outfielders this means hitting the cut off guy, vocally communicating in the outfield, making normal catches. I'm not concerned about range as much for right field and left field. I'll give up arm strength for baseball intelligence and fundamentals.

Every battle is won or lost in the preparation.
The Manager and players must be spending their down time in the preparation. These players are found by scouts and management through preparation, and developed in the organization through preparation.

Just as most games are not won or lost on the homerun, but instead on the cutoff missed, I believe teams are set up to win or lose on strong management models, scouting, player selection development, and the study of applicable, measurable sabermetrics that lead to educated risks on players.

Section 6 – Phillies Organization

Phillies Scouting and General Management

This section is extremely exciting because it provides real-world insight into the General Management and Scouting positions. The casual fan will gain interesting perspective and appreciation for what it takes to run a baseball team, and to identify, draft and groom baseball players.

I was quite fortunate to have been provided valuable time and insight into the Scouting and General Management roles by the Philadelphia Phillies Assistant General Manager (at the time of original printing), Ruben Amaro Jr., (now the Senior Vice President and General Manager) and the Assistant Scouting Director, Rob Holiday.

Both men took significant time from their schedules right before they were headed out to begin the spring training season in order to accept my request for interviews. The fact that they provided this much attention to my interviews speaks volumes about the class and professionalism they bring to the Phillies organization.

1. Phillies Scouting

As I listened to Rob Holiday, I recognized that his valuable insight into scouting management structure and grading philosophy supported and mirrored the MLB Scouting materials taught in the SMWW General Manager and Scouting Course.

The Organization Discipline and Philosophy

The Phillies have a long respected Scouting and Player Development organization. Leadership includes:
- Chuck Lamar - Assistant General Manager, Scouting and Player Development.

- Marti Wolever - Scouting Director. Marti is the ultimate draft choice decision maker.

- Rob Holiday - Assistant Scouting Director.

The organization structure is an established cross-check system:
- Organization cross-checks:
  - Domestic Scouting.
    - 2 National Scouting Coordinators.
    - 3 Regional Supervisors.
    - 16 Area Supervisors, plus free agent, territory, part time and associate scouts.
  - International coverage.
  - Professional coverage.
  - Latin Operations.
  - Minor league operations.
  - Computer Analysis.

- Grading cross-checks:
  - The Phillies organization utilizes the 40 to 80 based variation of the standard MLB Grading Scale.

- Players graded 50 or greater by Area Supervisors are cross checked by the Regional Supervisors, then by the National Scouting Coordinators and other direct contributors.

- Players graded 40-49 will not receive as much visibility to the higher organization levels.

- The organization is a highly respected organization of long-time scouting veterans (for example, Ruben Amaro Sr.) who sustain team scouting and development continuity.

- The Phillies train their own scouts. The team focuses training on the team philosophy and methodology for grading each player, determining sign ability, researching medical history, gathering biographies.

Player development standards for placement:
- High school (17-18 year olds) and international players – Gulf Coast League Phillies (R).
- Drafted players out of college (21-23 year olds) – Batavia Muckdogs (A).
- Minor League experienced - Lakewood BlueClaws (A).
- Higher Level of experience – Clearwater Threshers (A).
- Tougher jump is from A to AA – Reading Phillies (AA).
- Scranton/Wilkes-Barre Red Barons (AAA).

Prospects are defined by talent, makeup, and signability:

- Graded by tools for each field position, with an evolution of criteria over the years as the game changes.

  For example, today the scouts grade shortstops by hands, feet and arms (read *Dollar on the Muscle*, by Kevin Kerrane for grading by position).

- Thoroughly checked medical history. Cost of drafting a player is not just salary and bonus. Cost for surgical fees can be significant. The team reviews pitching style, delivery, and body type to predict how the body will hold up.

- Assessed for psychological makeup. Each prospect is given a test to determine his psychological profile.

- Projected by where they will fit into the organization (I.e. A, AA, AAA, etc.). Projection is calibrated yearly based upon the talent tools, development, adjustment to failure, and personal makeup.

- For hitters the Phillies look for bat speed, how ball jumps off of the bat, even in batting practice.

- For players in general, the Phillies want players with baseball "instincts" or "over-achievers."

- Players should have arm strength, and have strong, durable bodies for both health and season wear and tear.

Pitchers should be circa 6'5."

- Left handed pitchers can generally be shorter due to a more natural pitching movement.

- Pitchers should have a strong delivery with velocity on the pitches. A 2nd pitch is also assessed.

The Scouting Schedule

Scouting has amateur, professional and international areas of concern:
- Immediately after the yearly draft is over the team begins preparing for the next draft!

- A "follow list" is developed to track top prospects for each territory:
  - The list is revisited at the end of fall.
  - The list is revised again in December.

- January begins the scouting season.

- The budget is set by the CEO based on previous year draft results.

- The scouts cover colleges, high schools, any where there are leads.

- International scouting is on-going year round in other countries with players not included in the draft:
  - There are four full time scouts plus part-time scouts.
  - Part time scouting includes Taiwan, South Korea, Australia, and Europe including Czech Republic.
  - Video review of players is year-round.
  - The Phillies attend the yearly Australia tournament where the best 18-under Australians compete.

Professional scouts manage AA, AAA, player trades and released player evaluations.

Area Supervisors and independent scouts manage A level players.

Professional scouting coverage takes over after the player draft.

Scouting leadership maintains regular conference calls, updates, and face to face meetings.

2.   Phillies General Management

I gathered the information in this section through an interview with the Philadelphia Phillies Assistant General Manager, Ruben Amaro Jr. I greatly appreciate the time and insight Ruben provided in order to paint the bigger picture of General Management that casual baseball fans do not get to see.

Most fans think of the General Manager and Assistant General Manager roles only in terms of making player transactions. However, MLB General Management includes significant unheralded coordination of "corporate" responsibilities, and disciplines while maintaining budget constraints dictated by the team ownership.

In summary, the General Management and Scouting functions within Major League Baseball teams are12 month-per-year responsibilities. Attention to detail on a daily basis is essential or the team may be negatively impacted by any number of legal, financial, operation ways.

The General Management is responsible for player acquisition, philosophy and discipline, but even more for player management and relationships throughout the internal and external enterprise.

The MLB General Management is responsible for:

1. Handling talent, contracts and control, including:
   - Continual contact with the other MLB teams.

   - Relationships with agents.

   - MLB Players Relations Board.

   - Public Relations.

   - All contract negotiations.

   - Arbitration hearings.

   - Own team arbitrator.

   - Determine player transactions.

   - Weekly scouting and player development status.

   - Debrief leadership in monthly Vice-President meetings.

   - Media communications.

   - Debrief meetings with the legal department.

   - Manage the budget as defined by ownership.

   - Manage daily player and team issues.

2. Building a competitive team:
- Trade negotiations.

- Utilize internal proprietary team Sabermetrics tools for analysis.

- Player process blocking and claiming.

- Daily 4pm submit and monitor of the MLB transaction system known as EBIS.

- Utilize EBIS for player backgrounds, waivers, options and contracts.

- Continually monitor free agents, trade opportunities, player activity in other countries, the Phillies own organization and minor league system in order to always look for ways to improve the team.

3. Work within MLB established deadlines and milestones. Milestones announced yearly:

- June - Amateur draft.

- July - Last day to trade a player without securing waivers.

- September. - Active rosters expand to 40 players.

- October-November - Free agent filing period, first 15 days after World Series ends.

- November - GM meetings, Naples, Fla.

- December:
  - Winter meetings, Lake Buena Vista, Fla.

  - Major League Baseball Players Association executive board meeting.

  - Final day announced for teams to offer salary arbitration to their former players who became free agents.

  - Final day for free agents offered salary arbitration to accept or reject the offers.

  - Final day for teams to offer contracts to unsigned players.

- January:
  - Salary arbitration filings.

  - Last day until May 1 announced for free agents who rejected arbitration to re-sign with their former teams.

  - Exchange of salary arbitration figures.

- February:
  - Salary arbitration hearings.

  - Mandatory player reporting date.

- March:
  - Teams may renew contracts of unsigned players.

  - Final day to place a player on unconditional release waivers, 30 days termination pay vs. 45.

  - Final day to request unconditional release waivers on players without paying full salary.

- April - Opening day. Active rosters reduced to 25 players.

When meeting with the scouting and player development teams, the General Management team discusses players in terms of the guiding Phillies Draft Philosophy:

- Physical
  - Pitching is a priority
  - Best athlete
  - Fluidity
  - Footwork
  - Arm action
  - Arm speed
  - Down angle
  - Taller players
  - Bat speed and extension
  - Consistent hard bat-ball contact

- Player Mental Makeup
  - Psychological studies,
  - Can handle failure,
  - Can handle the Phillies market.

- Sabermetrics.
  - Priority on college players.
  - High school data less important

It was exciting having the interview with Ruben Amaro Jr. in his office because it looked like a war room. Ruben was informed of all free agents and player movement at all times, and he had the 40 man rosters for each team on a wall.

He had a color-coated magnet for each player:

- White for right handed pitchers.

- Orange for left handed pitchers.

- Yellow for left handed hitters.

- Blue for right handed hitters.

- Red for switch hitters.

Section 7 - Baseball Economics

Major League Baseball Economic Factors

STeeRIKE! Baseball players hear umpires make this familiar call many times per game. STRIKE! This strike call echoing through the summer winds, however, is the all too common call for work stoppage. As tensions get high there are passionate theories from owners, players and fans about who is at fault. Are the owners losing money or are the players being underpaid? Can player value even be measured? Much of the public debate on talk shows and in the media is ambiguous and passion driven. My aim is to recognize, for the court of public opinion, a foundation of six core considerations to better quantify the debate over the current economic state of Major League Baseball (MLB). The six core considerations are:

1. Are player contracts derivatives?
2. What is the key factor of production?
3. Can MLB Marginal Product of Labor be quantified contractually?
4. Is Economic Rent the key to player value?
5. Are owners monopsonists, player monopolists, or is the culture a bi-lateral monopoly?
6. Are exogenous variables essential factors in determining player worth?

1. Are player contracts derivatives?

Definition:

Derivative is a financial contract whose value depends on, or is derived from, an underlying asset. Types of derivatives include forwards, futures, swaps and options.

Assumptions:

- The player contracts can be bought, sold or traded in a competitive market. The contracts in this study are interpreted to be similar in nature to the markets where a person can negotiate futures or some other derivatives, with similar risks.
- The player's skill set is considered a quantifiable, underlying asset.

Most people argue that baseball players are either overpaid or underpaid. Perhaps the players are NEITHER overpaid nor underpaid. If players negotiate based upon the value of their underlying assets, plus their potential output from their skills, then the contracts can be viewed by definition as derivatives.

An argument against this view is that player talent is a homogeneous product with normal market risk factors. However, Major League Baseball (MLB) talent is neither homogeneous in quality nor are the contracts structured with enough safety valves to be considered normal. Baseball clubs invest heavily in thousands of ballplayers who never become productive members of the parent ball club. Also, while the aggregate propensity in many player statistics from year to year can fluctuate enormously, there is a high percentage of guaranteed (no restrictions) contracts in MLB. Under these conditions, it is interpreted that teams take greater risks than most firms.

Further examining the derivatives theory, a player and an owner sign a financial contract whose value depends on, or is derived from, the underlying asset of the player's baseball abilities (potential value) and/or potential revenue drawing power. Similar to an investor gambling on commodity futures (some may say like gambling at a craps table), the owner and player each gamble that the player will perform as expected. The owner may gamble that:

- The player will produce at the expected level.
- The player will produce for the life of the contract.
- The player will not publicly deface the integrity of MLB, the ball club or the city.
- The player may gamble that:
  - He will not exceed his expected output, based on his evaluation of his skills.
  - He will produce at least to the level expected of him so that he can negotiate a favorable contract in the future.

Answer # 1:

Are player contracts derivatives? Although specific motives vary, both parties expect to prosper from the underlying potential skill asset. There is enough substance to the "derivatives" theory that it should be considered a viable alternative to contemporary views.

Impact:

Regardless of the public debates each team and each player enters into individual MLB contractual agreements based upon their own judgments of value, risk and reward in relation to their overall portfolio.

2. What is the Key Factor of Production?

Definition:
Factor of production is an input used to produce goods and services; for example, capital labor.

Assumptions:

- $Y = (K, L)$;
  Y = total output. K = total capital. L = total labor.

- **Labor drives baseball-media contracts.** Cable technology, internet and other factors significantly add profits and capital investment to teams and fund new ballparks. However, if the player labor quality decreased to average or below levels, then capital and fans would move to other baseball leagues or sports. Cable and network television money would also decrease.

Labor is the overwhelmingly dominant factor of production. The input of player baseball skills produces the key output; wins, losses, pennants, championships, fan excitement, revenue or whatever output is deemed important by the interpreter. The view that owner investment is a factor of capital and revenue output, generated through team oriented patents, concessions, television revenues, etc., (regardless of the specific players) is a viable one. However, whether the desired output is wins or revenue, there usually is a direct correlation between player productivity to wins and revenue.

Answer #2:

What is the key factor of production? Labor is the key factor of production.

Impact:

Unlike some other sports leagues, MLB players and their union control the salary ranges. Replacement players at a comparable level are not available so ultimately, including work stoppages, the players are only limited by their perseverance and the strength of the economy.

Owners balance the labor costs with capacity planning, corporate sales, yield management, media and other fiscal disciplines out of competitive necessity. At the end of the day, the economy invisible hand will make upward and downward corrections to salaries.

Interestingly, since the economy is stronger or weaker city by city, this judgment validity is reinforced by the salary ranges of teams in each small, medium and large market.

3.   Can MLB Marginal Product of Player Labor be quantified contractually?

Definition:

Marginal Product of Labor is the amount of extra output produced when labor input is increased by one unit.

Assumptions:

- Baseball is a competitive market of teams.
- One season. The player value of MPL is evaluated one complete season at a time.
- Sticky prices. The value of the wage is given and remains constant during the course of one season.
- Maximizing teams. The theory that baseball is more than one hundred years old because MLB has practiced profit maximization is accepted as fact.
- There are two dominant maximization oriented philosophies among teams today:
  1. Profit maximizers. These are teams built on economic efficiency of labor and revenue units.
  2. Victory maximizers. Owners whose interpretation of efficiency and profit is determined by the labor costs versus production of championship units.

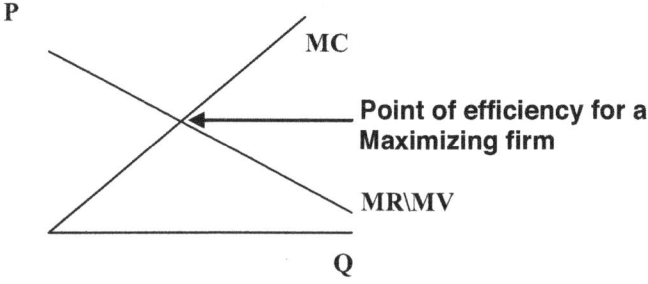

P

MC

Point of efficiency for a
Maximizing firm

MR\MV

Q

Profits are maximized when:
Marginal Revenue, or to some owners, Marginal Victory = Marginal
Cost

IN RELATION TO LABOR		L	= labor
W = VMP = MPP * P		W	= wages of labor
VMP = W		P	= price
MPP * P = W	WHERE	MPP	= marginal physical product of labor
P = W / MPP		VMP	= value marginal product of labor
MR = MC			

From a supply-demand perspective, MLB pays the players the Value of Marginal Product of their labor because:

- There is a fixed supply of quality players (scarce resources).
- The factor of labor is unresponsive to price because there is a fixed supply.
- The demand by the owners for each player exceeds the supply (all but one team wish that they had the player(s) that would have made them the best, or produced additional revenue, or both).
- Most owners believe there is a direct correlation between quality players, winning, and revenues

Since the supply of the available players is fixed, the position of the demand curve determines the price that each player will be paid.

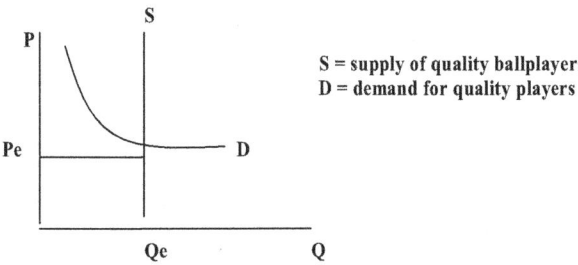

Not everyone agrees that the players are paid the value of MPL in the "real world." For example, unions gained power at a time when **VMP > W**. Proponents of this assumption theorize that other market conditions artificially raise or lower employee salaries. They also either disagree with the methods used to quantify exact player values, or they agree to the same models as viable tools but utilize different exogenous assumptions to support their views. This gets complicated so let's take a closer look at the factors argued regarding baseball value maximization:

a. Complications for quantifying profit maximization by specific player value.

The dominant solution argued by those advocating payment-by-MPL, is to place values squarely on direct player statistics. It would seem relatively easy to establish the standard value of MPL for players if revenue could be defined as the output. Pedro Martinez, for example, might theoretically be measured by attendance on all days he did not pitch against each opponent versus days he did pitch.

For nearly all other players, it is far more difficult, if not impossible, to accurately determine their direct revenue generating worth. Several examples;

- How many people went to Philadelphia games to see Ryan Howard, or Jimmy Rollins or Bobby Abreu? All three played for the Philadelphia Phillies. How many people went to see Bobby Abreu when he joined the Yankees? How many fans attend games to see the Phillies as a team or another team or a player on another team?

- How should days of the week or fan appreciation days be factored? How many go to see the ballpark? Wrigley Field, Chicago and Fenway Park, Boston both are usually near spectator capacity whether the teams are winning or not. Colorado years ago drew 70,000 - 80,000 fans per game and they had a losing record.

- How do customer businesses with team season tickets and suites factor into player value?

b. Complications for quantifying victory maximization by specific player value.

There is evidence that utilizing statistics to place "value standards" on player worth is theoretically possible as a general, comparative measure. Players, agents and owners use sabermetrics in negotiations and arbitration because the information is generally accepted as valuable.

However, the counter arguments are endless, starting with which statistics are relevant or even truly quantifiable? Potentially incomplete, inaccurate, differently interpreted or prejudiced assessment of player value can and will produce controversial results.

There is ample evidence that shows how difficult it is to quantify individual MR=MC in a team and market driven sport. Evidence does not support placing precise value on an individual independent of the overall team. Much of what constitutes value to a team effort is not reflected in individual statistics. There is a saying, "you have white lies, you have lies, and then you have statistics." Even when otherwise utilized efficiently, use of statistics as an arbitration tool is faulty due to legal skewing of statistical interpretation.

Answer # 3:

Can Marginal Product of Labor be quantified contractually?
In theory, MPL could be quantified in general but the ground rules would need to be negotiated by the owners and players' union. This will never happen. Even from a unified baseline, the power struggle to dominate the yearly calibration of determining MPL would be disastrous.

Team ownerships are split between revenue and victory maximizers so they do not have a unified stand against the profit maximizing players and union. Additionally, there historically have been various levels of splits between baseball union members; natural splits exist between the wealthy players and the second tier players. Realistically, giving a player a raise solely because his stats are better than another, within a team sport, is not viable. Additionally, what about multi-year contracts? Enormous obstacles exist.

In practice the model is flawed. Artificial salary expectations are not viable. Players may or not be underpaid by definition but it's a team game. You can't play by yourself. There are so many variables that VMP cannot be measured accurately.

Impact:

There is no concrete reason for players or the teams to institutionalize MPL to contracts. This, to me as a supply-sider, would be like moving from a free market to socialism. Major League Baseball will survive without quantifying MPL for standard contracts.

4.   Is Economic Rent the key to player value?

Definition:

Economic rent is said to be earned whenever a factor of production receives a reward that exceeds the minimum amount necessary to keep the factor in its present employment.

Assumptions:

- Answer # 1 above - the key factor of production is labor.
- Answer # 2 above - contracts are derivatives.
- Answer # 3 above – MPL may be quantified contractually in theory but not in reality of a free market.
- Competition is a key to player value.
- Team profit is a key to player value.
- Intangible value set by owners, fans, managers and players is a moving key to player value.
- Potential competition from other leagues is a key to player value.
- Labor strength may set the bar for minimum rewards but the labor strength is earned as the key factor of production value.

Owners have not been unified enough in the past to test the theoretical level of player economic rent. If economic rent is prevalent in MLB it would be due to the struggle between the victory maximizers and profit maximizers. Owners who victory-maximize are said to pay players vastly more for the players' skills than the players would have accepted, their economic rent. The profit maximizing teams, being price takers, are then forced in future negotiations and arbitration hearings to offer comparable contracts.

Three considerations:

- Every team could, if desired, sign a team of league minimum salaries. No team signs every player at league minimum because there are various tangible and intangible levels of success expectations for every team. Since MLB is a competitive free market, then in general players are paid what the open market will bear.

- If a team signs a player at a price that no other team would pay in order to meet their defined success factors, then that team paid an economic rent to the player. A majority of players would need to be paid under this scenario in order for this to be the key player value.

- Even if a handful of victory-maximizing teams pay some of their players more than necessary simply because they are richer than other teams, there are still too many players and teams in competition paying market rates to define economic rent as the key to player value. Player values have been perceived to be artificially high yearly since the 1970s but the competitive market continues to drive the value equilibrium.

Although many players signed do not live up to expectations and teams do not attain the expected value, there is no evidence that any team, as business practice, pay excessive economic rent. Keep in mind that on each team there are also many players who out perform higher priced counterparts. That is why the Yankees do not win every year.

Answer # 4:

Is Economic Rent the key to player value? Although there are examples of some perceived instances that players may be paid an economic rent, competition in a free market with various expectations of successes are what determine player salaries in general. Economic rent is not the key player value.

Impact:

Owners may pay more for players than they would like but MLB is not overrun by economic rent. MLB minimum salaries will continue to be calibrated by economic forces and competition.

5. Are owners Monopsonists, players Monopolists, or bi-lateral monopoly?

Definitions:

- Monopsony refers to a market situation in which there is only one buyer.
- A pure monopoly is an industry in which there is only one supplier of a product for which there are no close substitutes, and in which it is very hard or impossible for another firm to coexist.
- A bilateral monopoly is a market situation in which there is both a monopoly on the selling side and a monopsony on the buying side.
- MLC is the marginal labor costs.
- MRP is the marginal revenue product.

Assumption - A union shop is an arrangement under which non-union workers may be hired, but then must join the union within a specified period of time.

There is sentiment that owners enjoy the benefits of being monopsonists. At first glance, this could be correct when accepting that individual teams have the rights to baseball players during the initial years of the players' major league careers. This theory proposes that the owners are able to keep the wages below the market clearing (equilibrium) price. Some players, agents and economists have been quoted saying that the players are subjected to "seasons of servitude."

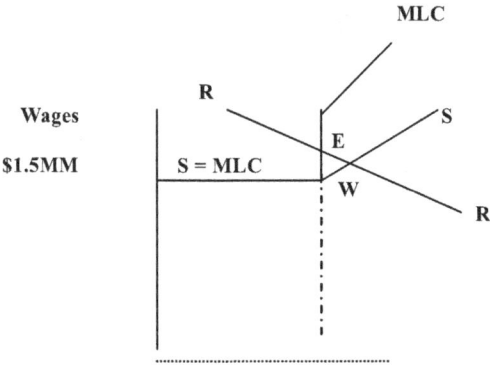

A UNION UNDER MONOPSONY
650 – number of workers

MLC is horizontal up to 650 players then jumps. This moves equilibrium employment to point E where 650 players are employed at $1.5 million. Compared with the adjoining graph, unions can raise both wages and employment.

****

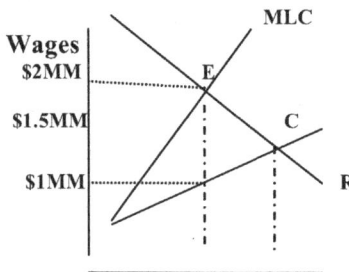

600   700   number of workers
LABOR MARKET UNDER MONOPSONY

The labor market equilibrium rate occurs at the employment level that equates MLC to the MRP. The equilibrium is at point E, where 600 players are employed at $1MM. In a competitive market, equilibrium would be at point C with 700 workers at wages at $1.75 million.

Generally owners argue that the system benefits the players. Owners would negotiate this servitude point with the players but the players ultimately do not want to lose this benefit. The teams pay tremendous amounts in bonuses and player development, even for injured players. Many players would be out of work or would be paid less if the structure was changed.

One theory is that players have damaged the stability of Major League Baseball because the world's most powerful monopoly seller of labor, the players union, has kept contracts above the market clearing price level. For this reason, the baseball players are able to keep the wages above the market clearing price.

If both arguments are accurate; if the owners are monopsonists and the players are monopolists, then Major League Baseball is driven by a bilateral monopoly. The talent level in MLB is generally accepted as the greatest in the world. Anyone who wishes to compete at this level can only join this league and must join the union.

Analysts find it very difficult to predict the market equilibrium in this type of market because the outcome depends on:

Power relative to the union vs. the owners. The union is arguably the most powerful union globally.

Negotiator skills and preparation. The players, arguably, have overwhelmingly defeated owners in the bargaining and arbitration processes.

Economic factors. The owners claim to be losing money but the players disagree.

- Other factors such as luck.

- If player salaries were kept artificially low, then players could go to Japanese or other leagues, or create new leagues that would give credibility over MLB. MLB today is considered the single source for the greatest level of talent and competition globally.

The evidence seems to show that if MLB is not a competitive market and if salaries have not settled at the market clearing price then the players currently hold an artificial advantage over the owners.

How do fans factor into the debate? Many people believe player contracts are the root cause for rising ticket prices and the average person can no longer afford to go. But fans continue to support teams in record numbers and all forms of revenue combined grow profits and franchise values. From an economic perspective, this condition may be explained by assuming:
- Players are paid their VMP

- Increased revenues in this multi-billion dollar industry triggers player contracts to rise.

- Contracts are included in the equation:

- **PROFIT = REVENUE - COST.**

Therefore, the players are being paid higher salaries because there is a market for higher prices and owners, being efficient are moving prices toward that demand.

Answer #5:
Are owners Monopsonists, players Monopolists, or is the culture a bi-lateral monopoly? Current evidence supports the perspective that baseball is a bi-lateral monopoly between players and owners.

Impact:
MLB will continue to be run as a business. Richer teams who choose to increase labor costs as a competitive victory advantage effort will continue to challenge smaller markets' yearly competitive disciplines. Smaller markets who receive tax checks from the richer teams but who do not reinvest the tax revenue on players will continue to contribute to competitive gaps. However, relative parity in competitive opportunity should continue successfully.

6. Are exogenous variables essential factors in determining player worth?

Let's use the movie Bang the Drum Slowly as a case study regarding the value of intangible baseball factors. In the movie, the baseball team began the season as a group of individuals concerned about individual statistics; a team without the on-field fundamental chemistry arguably essential to being a world champion. The players then found out that Bruce Pearson, the catcher, was going to die of cancer. They, without his knowledge or their realization, rallied behind him. They began to communicate and work together fundamentally as TEAMMATES, not individuals. This TEAM chemistry carried New York to the World Series.

Bruce Pearson provided intangible winning presence (input) in triggering team victories (output), and increased attendance and revenue (output), and therefore, should be measured, in theory, when determining his MPL. However, in reality, quantifying his value into endogenous results is not viable.

Answer #6:
Are exogenous variables essential factors in determining player worth? Yes. This example highlights the limitations to including exogenous variables when developing a standard model for negotiating individual player contracts. "Bang the drum slowly" when considering whether or not each contract proposal on an individual basis is fair.

Impact:

Exogenous variables will always keep baseball in the business of baseball. As the yearly national past time from when there is still snow on the ground in some cities, through the spring and long dog days of summer, to the fall, when snow is beginning to fall again in those same cities, baseball is the game of endurance. Lives take many turns during the course of each year. No matter how many ways the game is redefined as business on steroids – eh, er, uh, bad example – as a super business, exogenous variables will create the people stories and game surprises that drive the passion in baseball fans.

7.   Final Verdict

Issue	Ruling	Favor Players	Favor Owners	Impact
1 Are player contracts derivatives?	Yes	X	X	Each team and each player enters into individual MLB contractual agreements based upon their own judgments of value, risk and reward in relation to their overall portfolio.
2 What is the key factor of production?	Labor	X		Players are only limited by their perseverance and the economy. The free market will make salary corrections separately in each small, medium and large market.
3 Can Marginal Product of Labor be quantified contractually?	No	X		Players will continue to be paid what the market can accept. Individual contracts will be set like derivatives. Free market works.
4 Is Economic Rent the key to player value?	No	X	X	MLB minimum salaries will continue to be calibrated by the economic forces and competition.
5 Are owners Monopsonists, players Monopolists, or Bi-lateral Monopoly?	Bi-lateral monopoly	X	X	MLB will continue to be run as a business. Relative parity in competitive opportunity should continue successfully.
6 Are exogenous variables essential factors in determining player worth?	Yes	X		Exogenous variables will always keep baseball game in the business of baseball. Fans will embrace the business as a game due to the individual achievements.

The Recap:

Baseball is a continual business work in progress but it successfully operates under a free market system that favors the players from a strength perspective in a healthy economy.

In Summary... Working Model vs. Random Walk

I believe that a Major League Baseball organization may find short term success through smart use of sabermetrics, a large cash flow, or combination of sabermetrics and cash. However, I believe the successful working model for the Major League Baseball general management is a toolkit that combines the sabermetrics and cash with organization discipline, strong baseball people and proven baseball strategy.

There is much current debate about the Oakland A's and other teams' successful use of sabermetrics to balance competition against wealthier teams. Perhaps lost in the debate is that all teams utilize some form of sabermetrics in their decision making process.

I believe, when defining the business of baseball, sabermetrics should be linked to an academic term used in business schools, often associated with the stock market. The term is *"random walk"* which essentially states that short-run changes in stock prices cannot be predicted based upon past actions.

In baseball terms, I strongly value utilizing some sabermetrics applications (especially the way Earl Weaver used to utilize information to predict and setup match-ups between the Orioles players against other opponents, while ignoring opposition data vs. non-Orioles opposition). I believe the data, when applied to on base percentage, banking on Pedro Martinez falling off a pitching cliff at 100 pitches, etc. can provide a competitive advantage.

However, teams without a disciplined management team, defined working model, and stable top-down organization philosophy, are essentially taking a random walk through the season when over-depending on sabermetrics choices in building a team. In other words, I believe that a team riding only on rotisserie use of sabermetrics to determine a successful roster would be quite disappointed by the team chemistry and on-the-field results. The extreme strategy of selecting a roster as though it is a rotisserie league or counting on less dependable data (such as batting average instead of on base percentage, etc.) will struggle.

Additionally, teams that choose to minimize salaries through sabermetrics will perpetually struggle through seasonal random walks and instability because richer teams are using forms of sabermetrics too. I believe that, of the two most sabmetric-centric teams, the Red Sox will beat the A's most of the time due to their cash and management.

From a potential player transaction perspective, I trust player bat speed, foot speed, physical and mental makeup, ability to adjust to the strike zone and pitches, application of fundamentals (hits the cutoff guy, makes wise running decisions, etc.) as well as baseball statistical intelligence because of the random walk intangibles and chance built into the game.

Most experts generally accept that a roster made up 100% of league minimum salary talent would win approximately 48 games. If accurate, this reinforces how MLB is a league of fragile competitive percentage point differentials. Just as MLB classically grades individual players by 5 tool skill-sets, I believe competitive advantage at the organization level takes more than sabermetrics and cash.

A team must have a clear, disciplined business model that links strong baseball and business people with proven philosophies from the ownership to the General Management to the Scouting department to the Development department to the field Manager and coaches to the players on the field. A break down in any area places stress on the other organization disciplines.

With each discipline in place, the ownership needs to provide the reinforcement of flexibility to the fiscal discipline. Ownership needs to calibrate risk expectations to determine how to reinforce General Management, Scouting and Field Management success with additional valued derivative contracts.

Appendices

Appendix A: Baseball Library

For insight into detailed use of sabermetrics, as well as books on baseball strategy, history, business of baseball, scouting, and up-to-date research, below are books that I maintain in my library:

- **Sabermetrics**
  - *The Numbers Game,* Alan Schwarz. My favorite reading. Details the history of the evolving baseball statistics.
  - *Baseball Prospectus,* BP Team of Experts on Baseball Talent. Yearly publication.
  - *The Scouting Notebook,* Sporting News and Stats Inc. Yearly publication.
  - *Mathematician at the Ballpark,* Ken Ross. Odds and probabilities for fans.
  - *Bill James Historical Baseball Abstract,* Bill James. (read any book by Bill James)
  - *Minor League Baseball Analyst,* Deric Mckamey. Fully integrates sabermetrics and scouting by a Scout.
  - *Baseball Hacks,* Joseph Adler. Manual for research and analyze baseball data.
  - *Neyer/James Guide to Pitchers,* Bill James and Rob Neyer. Historical breakdown of pitchers, what they threw and insightful notes.
  - *Baseball between the Numbers,* Baseball Prospectus Team of Experts. These guys are great!

- **Scouting:**
  - *Baseball Uncensored,* Jonathan Story. Detailed lessons on how to grade and draft players as a professional scout.
  - *Dollar on the Muscle,* Kevin Kerrane. Explains the evolution of scouting through the baseball eras to today.

- **Game situational sabermetrics**
  - *Curve Ball,* Jim Albert and Jay Bennett. Statistics and the role of chance in the game. Gives insight into Sports Illustrated Baseball, Strat-O-Matic, APBA, ASB models.
  - *Weaver on Strategy,* Earl Weaver with Terry Pluto. The laws as written by Earl Weaver.
  - *3 Nights in August,* Buzz Bissinger. Insight from Tony LaRussa as the Cardinals Manager.
  - *The Bill James Guide to Baseball Managers: From 1870 to Today,* Bill James.

- **General Management**
  - *Moneyball,* Michael Lewis. Billy Beane is credited with for the A's successful through sabermetrics and little cash.
  - *Mind Game,* the writers of Baseball Prospectus. How Leo Epstein, Bill James and others used statistics and a blue print to win it all.
  - *Built to Win: Inside Stories and Leadership Strategies from Baseball's Winningest GM,* John Schuerholz, and Larry Guest. How John Schuerholz, with anti-Moneyball philosophies kept the Braves a winner.
  - *Winners: How Good Baseball Teams Become Great Ones (And It's Not the Way You Think),* Dayne Perry. Looks at the teams that made the playoffs over the past 26 years.
  - *The Book on the Book,* Bill Felber. Strategies, risk, reward and value on and off the field.
  - *The Tipping Point: How Little Things Can Make a Big Difference,* Malcom Gladwell. The smallest things can trigger enormous change.

I also visit the websites below to remain up-to-date on baseball activity:

- *mlb.com* – significant site for baseball statistics, transactions, news, streaming media.
- *Scout.com* – excellent coverage of minors, draft, teams.
- *Foxsports.com* – big news, rumors.
- *ESPN.com* – big news, editorials.
- *mlbcontracts.blogspot.com* – great site for detailed salary and contract information.
- *Online team city newspapers* – for example, nypost.com, dallasmorningnews.com, etc.
- *mlb4u.com/freeagent.php* – unofficial site to track free agents and arbitration.
- *Forbes.com* – strong reputation and valuable insight.
- *baseball-reference.com* – great insight into all areas of baseball.
- *http://www.maurybrown.com* - **Maury Brown** is the founder and president of the **Business of Sports Network,** which includes **The Biz of Baseball, The Biz of Football The Biz of Basketball and The Biz of Hockey**. He is also an author for **Baseball Prospectus, Basketball Prospectus** and is an available writer for other media outlets.

Appendix B: Paul Martino Sports Business Qualifications

Global corporate management, including sports, is a $multi-million high stakes, high pressure, and publicly visible culture.

Currently a corporate leader for a Global 500 corporation, I proved myself countless times under the gun with hands-on management leadership positions across industries globally for the past 25 years.

I also gained 17 baseball seasons of baseball culture and environment experience in sports reporting, working with the sports media, and working around baseball players and team management on game-days. Direct experience included game day sports statistician and reporter for ESPN Sports Ticker, covering the New York Yankees, New York Mets, and previously the Texas Rangers. Additionally, I managed the now highly valuable technology of media Internet portals and publishing.

SMWW (Sports Management World Wide) Certificates:
Baseball GM & Scouting
Training included: MLB collective bargaining agreement, sabermetrics, MLB scouting techniques, scouting reports, draft analysis, player evaluation, MLB general manager practices and statistical analysis formulas.

Hockey GM & Scouting
Training included: NHL and international scouting techniques, NHL and minor league hockey general manager practices, Rinknet Scouting Software, NHL collective bargaining agreement and statistical analysis.

Sport Business Management
Training included learning sports marketing best practices including: B2B and B2C sales, marketing, community relations, communications, branding, promotions and client services.
Reference: Dr. Lynn Lashbrook, President, Sports Management Worldwide, 503-445-7105 regarding SMWW courses and philosophy.

The following page provides additional insight that represents 25 years experience leading multi-million dollar, international, business mergers and initiatives within and in partnership with Sales, Marketing, Operations, HR, Finance, Legal, IT, and other enterprise entities.

Readiness Criteria	Readiness RYG	Demonstrated Skill and Experience
Corporate Leader	25 years experience managing corporate revenues and costs:	☑ Director of Americas at Global 500 company. ☑ Led Revenue Management, IS, Marketing, Operations, Sales, Delivery, Finance, HR, Communications, and Strategy stakeholders efforts. ☑ Led Global merger solutions.
Legal Contracts	17 years senior level experience crafting legal agreements	☑ Craft and approve partner, contractor and client contracts. ☑ Experienced with labor, Letters of Engagement, services, partnership, technical, Statement of Work agreements.
Negotiator	17 years senior level negotiating $ multi-million deals.	☑ Negotiate and approve $multi-million labor, services, product deals. ☑ Consistently extend accounts and present new business cases through partner channels.
Global Competitor	Led business in Asia, Europe, and Americas for Global 1000.	☑ $50million direct successful annual sales commitments. ☑ Lead Global competitive strategy sessions. ☑ Deliver solutions for Global 1000 companies. ☑ 45 countries experience.
Leader of Teams	25 years leading winning teams across industries globally	☑ Leader of diverse Global large-scaled networked teams. ☑ Directly hire and manage all team individuals, for the successful delivery of $multi-million projects "wins."
Sports and Media	17 years MLB reporting Web portals experience	☑ Major League Baseball, ESPN reporter; player interviews, statistical tracking and research, game summaries, and transaction reporting. ☑ Managed Internet media news publishing portals. ☑ Sports Management World Wide (SMWW) MLB, SBM, Hockey GM Certificates.
Winning intangibles	Strong core values, ethics. 24/7 energy, enthusiasm, loyal, team player.	☑ Bachelor (MIS), MBA degrees with emphasis on international business. Earned while working full-time. ☑ Coach and mentor. Lead by "sense of ownership."

APPENDIX C:

Official Book on the Business of Baseball General Management
Testimonials & About the Author